Gong Donkeys

Richard Cameron

T0262451

Methuen Drama

Published by Methuen 2004

1 3 5 7 9 10 8 6 4 2

First published in 2004 by
Methuen Publishing Limited
215 Vauxhall Bridge Road
London SW1V 1EJ

Methuen Publishing Limited Reg. No. 3543167

A CIP catalogue record for this book is available
from the British Library

ISBN 0 413 77494 5

Typeset by Country Setting, Kingsdown, Kent

The Bush Theatre presents the world premiere of

GONG DONKEYS

By Richard Cameron

3 November - 11 December

thebushtheatre

Cast

(In order of appearance)

Uncle Robert	**Edward Peel**
David	**Rory Jennings**
Aunt Deelie	**Anita Carey**
Charlene	**Andrea Lowe**
Wink	**Burn Gorman**
Gobbo	**Peter Bramhill**
Director	**Mike Bradwell**
Designer	**Lisa Lillywhite**
Lighting Design	**Paul Russell**
Sound Design	**Scott George** for **Aura**
Deputy Stage Manager	**Nicole Keighley**
Assistant Stage Manager	**Alexa Vickery**
Press Representation	**Alexandra Gammie** 020 7833 2627
Graphic Design	**Cog Design** (www.cogdesign.com)
Photography	**Gordon Rainsford** (www.gordonrainsford.co.uk)
Fairground Location	**Irvin Leisure** (www.irvinleisure.co.uk)

Gong Donkeys received its world premiere at The Bush Theatre on 5th November 2004.

At The Bush Theatre

Artistic Director	**Mike Bradwell**
Executive Producer	**Fiona Clark**
General Manager	**Brenda Newman**
Literary Manager	**Nicola Wilson**
Marketing Manager	**Gillian Jones**
Production Manager	**Pam Vision**
Technical Manager	**Matt Kirby**
Resident Stage Manager	**Ros Terry**
Literary Assistant	**Holly Hughes**
Assistant General Manager	**Nic Wass**
Box Office Supervisor	**Dominique Gerrard**
Box Office Assistants	**Rowan Bangs**
	Amanda Wright
Front of House Duty Managers	**Adrian Christopher**
	Sarah Hunter
	Lois Tucker
	Catherine Nix-Collins
	Sarah O'Neill
Associate Artists	**Tanya Burns**
	Es Devlin
Sheila Lemon Writer In Residence	**Jennifer Farmer**

The Bush Theatre continues to develop its Writers Development Programme with the generous support of the Peggy Ramsay Foundation Award 2002

The Bush Theatre
Shepherds Bush Green
London W12 8QD

The Alternative Theatre Company Ltd. (The Bush Theatre)
is a Registered Charity number: 270080
Co. registration number: 1221968
VAT no. 228 3168 73

Peter Bramhill Gobbo

Peter trained at the Welsh College of Music and Drama.

Theatre credits include *Othello* (RSC & Trafalgar Theatre), *Lady Windemere's Fan* (English Theatre Frankfurt), *Macbeth* (Ludlow Festival), *Corpus Christi* (Theatre 28), Switchboard (Pluto Productions), *A Chirstmas Carol* (Birmingham Rep), *As You Like It* (Theatre Royal Bath & Tour), *Anthony & Cleopatra* (Theatre Royal Bath & Tour) and *Strangers In The Night* (Salisbury Playhouse).

Television credits include *Footballers Wives* (Shed Productions).

Film credits include *The Nuggett Run* (Zig-Zag Films), *Jump* (Silver Films), *Loveroy* (Rawfilm), *Human Traffic* (Fruit Salad Films) and *Festival* (Festival Films).

Anita Carey Aunt Deelie

Anita trained at the Central School of Speech and Drama.

Anita's London theatre credits include *Star Gaze Pie* and *Sauerkraut* (The Royal Court Upstairs), *Other Worlds* (The Royal Court), *Hobson's Choice* (The Haymarket), *Semi Detached* (Greenwich), *Soundings* (Old Red Lion) and *Under The Web* (Soho Poly).

Anita's regional theatre credits include *Habeas Corpus* (Royal Theatre, Northampton), *The Importance of being Earnest* (The Watermill, Newbury), *Death of a Salesman* and *Misalliance* (Birmingham Rep), *Who's Afraid of Virginia Woolf?* (Nottingham Playhouse and Colchester), *Shirley Valentine* (The Swan, Worcester), *A Mongrel's Heart* (Lyceum, Edinburgh), *Richard III* (Northern Broadsides), *Sisters* and *Guys and Dolls* (Royal Exchange).

Television series and serials include *The Murder Room* (BBC), *Heartbeat* (Yorkshire), *Rescue Me* (Tiger Aspect), *Band of Gold, Spoils of War* and *First Among Equals* (Granada), *A Kind of Living* (Central), *Last of the Summer Wine, I Didn't Know You Cared, Ripping Yarns, Oneupmanship, Whatever Happened to the Likely Lads* (BBC).

TV plays and Films include *Wyvern Mysteries, Some Enchanted Evening* and *Fred Freud Is Dead* (Granada), *Perfect Strangers, Collision Course, Frankie and Johnny, Cries From A Watchtower, Ladies, Something's Wrong, Mr and Mrs Bureaucrat* and *Joey* (BBC). Anita's most recent film credit is *Still Crazy*.

Burn Gorman Wink

Previously at The Bush; *The Green Man* (Bush Theatre/Plymouth). Other recent theatre includes *Flush* (Soho Theatre Company), *Ladybird* (Royal Court), *Tiny Dynamite* (Frantic Assembly/Paines Plough), and studio and development work with The Royal Court, National Theatre, Soho Theatre, Young Vic and Royal Exchange.

Television credits include *Inspector Lynley Mysteries* (BBC), *The Shoreditch T**t* (Talkback Productions), *A Good Thief* (Granada), *Mersey Beat* (BBC), *Casualty* (BBC) and *Coronation Street* (Granada).

Film credits include *The Best Man, Colour Me Kubrick, Red Light Runners, Layer Cake, The Bully Boys, Love Is Not Enough, Runners* and *Van Boys.*

Burn has worked extensively on radio, most recently as Sam Weller in *The Pickwick Papers* for BBC4, and as a musician with various artists, including Neneh Cherry, Groove Armada and Fatboy Slim.

Rory Jennings David

Rory trained at the Sylvia Young Theatre school. His theatre credits include *Transgression* (National Theatre).

Television credits include *Urban Gothic* (Urban Gothic Prods), *Randall and Hopkirk* (Ghost Productions), *The Wings of Angels* (BBC), *The Affair* (Anglia/HBO), *Watch* (Spelthorne Prod/BBC), *Casualty* (BBC), *The Fast Show* (BBC) and *Tom's Midnight Garden* (BBC).

Film credits include *The People's Princess* (Parma Pictures), *Mary Shelley's Frankenstein* (Columbia Tristar) and *Fatherland* (HBO).

Radio credits include *Just Prose* (BBC Radio 3) and *Feelings Under Siege* (BBC Northern Ireland).

Andrea Lowe Charlene

Theatre credits include *Bash* (Citizens Theatre Glasgow), *A Day In Dull Armour* (Royal Court Theatre Upstairs), *The Birthday Party* (Crucible Theatre Sheffield) and *Lost and Found* (River House Barn).

Television credits include *A Thing Called Love* (BBC), *Murder City* (Granada), *No Angels* (World Productions/Channel 4), *Rescue Me* (Tiger Aspect for BBC), *Fields of Gold* (BBC), *Night and Day* (BBC), *Peak Practice* (Carlton), *The Bill* (Pearson), *Sleeper* (BBC), *Doctors* (BBC) and *Nature Boy* (BBC).

Film credits include *Repeat After Me* (Channel 4 Dogma Series; Ideal World), *The Rover's Return* (Short End Films), *Club Le Monde* (Screen Production Associates), *Pandaemonium* (Mariner Films), *The Perfect G* (London Guildhall), *Threesome* (Sugar & Water Films), *The Token King* (Channel 4) and *Snorted* (Goldsmiths College).

Edward Peel Uncle Robert

Edward Peel was born in Bradford, Yorkshire and has worked as an actor/director since 1966. He has appeard twice before at The Bush Theatre in *Pillion* by Paul Copley and *Sugar Sugar* by Simon Bent. He has recently worked with The Oxford Playhouse appearing as Serjeant Musgrave in *Serjeant Musgrave's Dance* by John Arden, and playing Manek in *Singer* by Peter Flannery at the Tricycle. His recent television work includes *Clocking Off, Cracker, Hillsborough* and Commander John Coleman in *London's Burning.*

Richard Cameron Writer

Gong Donkeys is Richard's sixth world premiere at The Bush, his previous plays here being *Pond Life, Not Fade Away, The Mortal Ash, All Of You Mine* and *The Glee Club*.

Richard has written for the Royal National Theatre (*Almost Grown*), Birmingham Rep (*Seven*), Belgrade Coventry (*In Bed With Billy Cotton*), West Yorkshire Playhouse (*With Every Beat*, written with the 1995 Thames Television Writer In Residence Award), and the Cambridge Theatre, West End (*Great Balls Of Fire*). His earlier work includes *Can't Stand Up For Falling Down, The Moon's Madonna* and *Strugglers*.

Richard's television work includes *Stone Scissors Paper*, with Ken Stott and Juliet Stevenson, winner of the inaugural Dennis Potter Award (BBC1), and an adaptation of the Berlie Docherty novel *Dear Nobody* (BBC).

Radio credits include *Heaven's Walk* (BBC Radio 4), *In The Bosom Of The Slag* (BBC Radio 4) and *The Kon-Tiki 2 Expedition* (BBC Radio 4), winner of the Mental Health Media Award, Radio Drama, 2003.

Richard is currently working on a Radio 4 commission, *Lessons for the Loveless*, a new play for Graeae Theatre, and an episode of *Midsomer Murders*.

Mike Bradwell Director

Mike trained at E15 Acting School and is Artistic Director of The Bush Theatre. He played Norman in Mike Leigh's award winning film *Bleak Moments* and was an actor/musician with The Ken Campbell Road Show and an underwater escapologist with *Hirst's Carivari*.

Mike founded Hull Truck Theatre Company in 1971 and directed all their shows for 10 years, including his own plays *Oh What, Bridget's House, Bed Of Roses, Ooh La La!, Still Crazy After All These Years* and news plays by Doug Lucie, Alan Williams and Peter Tinniswood. Mike has directed 35 shows at The Bush including *Hard Feelings* by Doug Lucie, *Unsuitable for Adults* by Terry Johnson, *The Fosdyke Sagas* by Bill Tidy and Alan Plater, *Love and Understanding* by Joe Penhall (also at The Long Wharf Theatre, U.S.A), *Love You, Too* by Doug Lucie, *Dead Sheep* and *Shang-a-Lang* by Catherine Johnson (also 1999 national tour), *Howie The Rookie* by Mark O'Rowe (also Civic Theatre, Tallaght and Andrew's Lane theatres, Dublin, 1999 Edinburgh Festival, Plymouth Theatre Royal, The Tron, Glasgow, PS122 New York and the Magic Theatre, San Francisco), *Dogs Barking* by Richard Zajdllic, *Normal* by Helen Blakeman, *Resident Alien* by Tim Fountain (also for New York Theater Workshop), *Flamingos* by Jonathan Hall, *Blackbird* by Adam Rapp, *Little Baby Nothing* by Catherine Johnson, *Airsick* by Emma Frost, *adrenalin...heart* by Georgia Fitch (also at the Tram Theatre, Tokyo) and *The Glee Club* by Richard Cameron (also at The Duchess Theatre 2002 and at Bolton Octagon Galway Arts Festival and on tour in 2004).

Mike has also directed new plays by Helen Cooper, G.F Newman, Jonathan Gems, Richard Cameron, Flann O'Brien and Terry Johnson at Hampstead Theatre, the Tricycle, King's Head, West Yorkshire Playhouse, Science Fiction Theatre of Liverpool, The National Theatre of Brent, The Rude Players of Winnipeg and The Royal Court, where he was Associate Director.

Mike has written and directed for television including *The Writing on the Wall, Games Without Frontiers, Chains of Love* and *Happy Feet* (BBC Screen One).

Lucy Foster Assistant Director

Lucy recently graduated from Oxford University, where she was President of Oxford University Drama Society. While there she directed new writing, the devised piece *Crossed Wire*, and Sarah Kane's *Crave*, which was selected for the 2002 National Student Drama Festival. *Crave* won a Judge's Individual Award and the assistant directing placement at The Bush. Since graduating, Lucy has assisted on a scratch performance of *Newsnight the Opera* at Battersea Arts Centre, worked with Mike Bradwell on *Nine Parts of Desire* at The Bush, and worked as assistant director to Mike Bradwell on *Airsick* and to Hettie Macdonald on *M.A.D.* both at The Bush Theatre.

Lisa Lillywhite Designer

Lisa was awarded the Arts Foundation Scenography Award in 2001. For The Bush, Lisa has designed *Got To Be Happy, Blackbird* and *A Carpet, A Pony and A Monkey*.

Other Design credits include *Blenheim Palace Music Festival 2004* (Andrew Miller Promotions), *The Lisbon Traviata* (King's Head), *Tape* (Soho Theatre), *Live from Golgotha* and *PWA: The Diaries of Oscar Moore* (both for the Drill Hall), *Young Hamlet* (Young Vic Theatre), *Modern Love* (Queen Elizabeth Hall), *The Changeling* (Southwark Playhouse), *Musical Youth* (Birmingham Rep Studio), *Dutchman* (Camden Etcetera), *Prometheus In Evin* and *Brighton Beach Scumbags* (both for the Brockley Jack).

Art Direction credits include *Smash Hits, Miss World, Mobo Awards, Pepsi Chart, Wicked Women* and *Classical Brits*.

www.lisalillywhite.co.uk

Paul Russell Lighting Designer

Most recently Paul has lit an Icelandic circus based version of *Romeo and Juliet* at the Young Vic.

Recent Lighting Design includes: *Four Knights From Knaresborough* (West Yorkshire Playhouse); *Mother Teresa Is Dead* and *Herons* both for Royal Court Theatre Upstairs; *Hard Times* at Newbury; the Royal National Theatre's International tour of *Closer*, including Prague and Moscow; *M.Butterfly* in Singapore; *Card Boys* at The Bush Theatre; and *The Way You Look Tonight* for Druid Theatre, Galway.

Other theatre includes *Exodus* (Tara Arts); *Martin & John* (Bush Theatre); *The Cherry Orchard* (Guildhall); *Danton's Death* (Gate Theatre); *Wishbones* (Bush Theatre); *Fat Janet* (Croydon Warehouse); *My Mother Said I Never Should* (Oxford Stage Co. and Young Vic); *The Wolves* (Paines Plough); *Peribanez* (Cambridge Arts); *Max Klapper, A Life In Pictures* (Electric Cinema, Portobello); *Buried Treasure* (Lyric); *The Eleventh Commandment* (Hampstead); *Iona Rains* (Croydon); *Exquisite Sister* (West Yorkshire Playhouse); *Not A Game For Boys* (Royal Court); *Yiddish Trojan Woman* (Cockpit); *All Of You Mine, Clocks And Whistles, Serving It Up, One Flea Spare, Trainspotting, In The Heart Of America, Democracy, The Chinese Wolf* and *Waiting At The Water's Edge* (Bush Theatre); *Silver Face, The Boat Plays, The Great Highway* and *Madness In Valencia* (Gate Theatre).

Opera includes: 2 one act operas for Spitalfields Opera; *Snatched By The Gods* and *Broken Strings* (Almeida), *Linda Di Chamonix* and *Rape Of Luctretia* (Guildhall), *Cosi Fan Tutti* (Ealing).

Paul is also Production Manager for the Young Vic Theatre, and previously was Production Manager for The Bush Theatre.

Scott George for Aura Sound Designer

Recent Sound Design credits include: (Associate Design) *Brighton Rock* (Almeida Theatre); *Three Women and A Piano Tuner, Cabaret* (Chichester Festival Theatre); (Associate Design) *Rattle Of A Simple Man* (West End); *adrenalin...heart* (The Bush Theatre); (Associate Design) *Jumpers* (Royal National Theatre/West End/Broadway); *The Good Intent* (Queen's Theatre, Hornchurch); *Us & Them, Fragile Land, The Safari Party* (Hampstead Theatre); (Associate Design) *Midnight's Children* (Royal Shakespeare Company); *Kosher Harry* (Royal Court); *Well Of The Saints, Playboy Of The Western World, Sharon's Grave, Sive* (Druid Theatre Company, Ireland); *Maria Friedman In Concert* (West End); *Taming of the Shrew* (Nottingham Playhouse); *Bollywood Jane, The Witches, Bali, Death of a Salesman* (Haymarket Theatre, Leicester); *Naked Talent Season* (The Bush Theatre).

Production Engineering credits include: *Benefactors* (Tour and West End); *Distance From Here* (Almeida); *Saturday Night Fever* (British Tour); *Lulu, Coriolanus/Richard II* (Almeida at Gainsborough Studios, New York and Tokyo); *Macbeth* (Royal Shakespeare Company tour); *Plenty* (Almeida at the Albery).

Scott is Show Control Director of London based Aura Sound Design Ltd, which was founded in January 1998.

The Bush Theatre

The Bush Theatre opened in April 1972 in the upstairs dining room of The Bush Hotel, Shepherds Bush Green. The room had previously served as Lionel Blair's dance studio. Since then, The Bush has become the country's leading new writing venue with over 350 productions, premiering the finest new writing talent.

"One of the most vibrant theatres in Britain, and a consistent hotbed of new writing talent."
Midweek magazine

Playwrights whose works have been performed here at The Bush include:
Stephen Poliakoff, Robert Holman, Tina Brown, Snoo Wilson, John Byrne,
Ron Hutchinson, Terry Johnson, Beth Henley, Kevin Elyot, Doug Lucie, Dusty Hughes, Sharman Macdonald, Billy Roche, Tony Kushner, Catherine Johnson, Philip Ridley, Richard Cameron, Jonathan Harvey, Richard Zajdlic, Naomi Wallace, David Eldridge, Conor McPherson, Joe Penhall, Helen Blakeman, Lucy Gannon, Mark O'Rowe and Charlotte Jones.

The theatre has also attracted major acting and directing talents including Bob Hoskins, Alan Rickman, Antony Sher, Stephen Rea, Frances Barber, Lindsay Duncan, Brian Cox, Kate Beckinsale, Patricia Hodge, Simon Callow, Alison Steadman, Jim Broadbent, Tim Roth, Jane Horrocks, Gwen Taylor, Mike Leigh, Mike Figgis, Mike Newell and Richard Wilson.

Victoria Wood and Julie Walters first worked together at The Bush, and Victoria wrote her first sketch on an old typewriter she found backstage.

In over 30 years, The Bush has won over one hundred awards and recently received The Peggy Ramsay Foundation Project Award 2002. Bush plays, including most recently *The Glee Club*, have transferred to the West End. Off-Broadway transfers include *Howie the Rookie* and *Resident Alien*. Film adaptations include *Beautiful Thing* and *Disco Pigs*. Bush productions have toured throughout Britain, Europe North America and Asia, most recently *Stitching, Adrenalin... Heart* (representing the UK in the Tokyo International Arts Festival, 2004) and *The Glee Club* (UK National Tour, Autumn 2004).

Every year we receive over fifteen hundred scripts through the post, and we read them all. According to The Sunday Times:

"What happens at The Bush today is at the very heart of tomorrow's theatre"

That's why we read all the scripts we receive and will continue to do so.

Mike Bradwell
Artistic Director

Fiona Clark
Executive Producer

Be There At The Beginning

The Bush Theatre is a writer's theatre - dedicated to commissioning, developing and producing exclusively new plays. Up to seven writers each year are commissioned and we offer a bespoke programme of workshops and one-to-one dramaturgy to develop their plays. Our international reputation of over thirty years is built on consistently producing the very best work to the very highest standard.

With your help this work can continue to flourish.

The Bush Theatre's Patron Scheme delivers an exciting range of opportunities for individual and corporate giving, offering a closer relationship with the theatre and a wide range of benefits from ticket offers to special events. Above all, it is an ideal way to acknowledge your support for one of the world's greatest new writing theatres.

To join, please pick up an information pack from the foyer, call 020 7602 3703 or email info@bushtheatre.co.uk

We would like to thank our current members and invite you to join them!

Rookies

Anonymous
Anonymous
David Brooks
Sian Hansen
Lucy Heller
Mr G Hopkinson
Ray Miles
Malcolm & Liliane Ogden
Clare Rich & Robert Marshall
Martin Shenfield
Loveday Weymouth

Beautiful Things

Alan Brodie
Clive Butler
Clyde Cooper
Patrick and Anne Foster
Vivien Goodwin
Sheila Hancock
David Hare
William Keeling
Adam Kenwright
Laurie Marsh
John Reynolds
Mr and Mrs George Robinson
Tracey Scoffield
Barry Serjent
Brian D Smith

Glee Club

Anonymous
The Hon Mrs Giancarla
Alen-Buckley
Jim Broadbent
Stephen Lovegrove and Kate Brooke
Nick Marston
Shirley Robson

Lone Star

Silver Star

Bronze Corporate Membership

Act Productions Ltd

Silver Corporate Membership

The Agency

Platinum Corporate Membership

Anonymous

Gong Donkeys

*The story of Charles Dickens,
Wilkie Collins and Ellen Ternan in Doncaster,
as told by the Catcher in the Rye, an SAS commando,
Charlene from Number 27, and her cousin David*

Characters

David   *He's fourteen. Public school, but it's still Doncaster outskirts, so not all that posh. He's shy. A bookworm. His dad's a doctor, his mother's a patient in the psychiatric ward of DRI. Normally they live in Bessacarr (a posh part of town). Right now, he's about to stay with:*

Aunt Deelie   *Around forty. Works at the Spar shop. Used to be a learning assistant at a special school. Had a hysterectomy in her early thirties. Certain neighbours believed it was because her husband had worn her out:*

Uncle Robert   *Around forty. Ex-railway engineer at 'the plant works'. Redundant in mid-1990s, odd jobs ever since. Currently unemployed after recent spell as pizza delivery man. Chip on his shoulder – believes he could have gone far with the right education. Skint. Right-wing. Self-taught. Recently involved in local history. Is writing a 'paper' about Dickens in Doncaster. He's got one daughter:*

Charlene   *Eighteen, largish. She thinks she's unattractive. Maybe she is. Goes to college – hair and beauty. She's very much into one particular soap and fancies one of the characters – to the extent that she dreams up scenarios which she can be part of, using:*

Wink   *He's anywhere between twenty and twenty-eight, but his mental age is around twelve. He wears glasses, maybe with one frosted lens. A beanpole, an SAS commando. His best mate is:*

Gobbo   *Again twenties going on ten. Went to the same special school as Wink. He's actually very good looking, a bit of an Adonis. One day he plans to be a Catcher in the Rye.*

Settings

Deelie's house: the front room of a scruffy council pre-fab in a rough part of Doncaster.

Waste land: a stretch of neglected allotments, unused for many years. Overgrown.

Time

Summer. Now.

Scene One

Aunt Deelie's *house.*

Evening, mid July. The front room of a council house. There are very few ornaments. The furniture old, worn out. There's no money in this house.

David, *fourteen, smartly dressed, stands by his suitcase.* **Aunt Deelie** *takes a backpack from him.* **Uncle Robert** *sits watching.*

Robert   You're a bookworm these days, I 'ear? What sort of books?

David   I like different sorts.

Robert   Adventure books?

David   Yes.

Robert   *Treasure Island?*

David   I don't think I know –

Robert   Conan Doyle? *The Lost World?*

(*To* **Aunt Deelie**.) Down from school for the summer hols, eh?

(*To* **David**.) Or is it up?

Schooldays, eh? Latin grammar. Good old Major Minor, what a wheeze. The science master is a German spy.

Sherlock 'olmes. You must've read 'im.

David   No.

Robert   What 'ave you read, then?

Deelie   They're young people's adventures, aren't they?

Robert   Read any Dickens?

David   I'm not sure.

Deelie   He likes books about now, not olden times. Don't you?

Robert   'Ow do you know? (*To* **David**.) They don't do classics at school any more, then?

David   I'm not sure.

Deelie   I don't think they do.

Robert   No. Well, they never at your place, that's true. (*To* **David**.) Bash Street. *Oliver Twist?*

David   Pardon?

Robert   Pease puddin' and saveloys.

Deelie   'Ave you 'ad any tea?

David   Yes, thanks.

Deelie   I can make you something?

David   I'm all right, thank you, Aunt Deelie.

Robert   Midnight feasts. Tuck and all that. Billy Bunter. *Boy's Own.* If we come down and find 'im in the fridge, we put it down to a nocturnal 'abit, eh?

Nicholas Nickleby.

David   Sorry?

Robert   I bet you didn't know Charles Dickens visited these parts ?

Deelie   Shall I make us a nice cup of tea?

Robert   'Lazy Tour of Two Idle Apprentices.' 'Eard of that?

David   No. (*To* **Aunt Deelie**.) No, thank you.

Robert   Ah. No. You won't 'ave, I can guarantee you that. There's not many as 'as. One of the few. Little gem, though. A most interestin' and revealin' record of a visit by the man 'imself to the St Leger races with his friend and fellow writer, Wilkie Collins. 'Eard of 'im?

David   No.

Robert   Wrote ghost stories. Very popular in the mid-eighteen 'undreds. Like ghost stories?

David   Actually, I do.

Robert   Ah. Well, then. Actually I might tell you the one 'e wrote set in a pub not very far from 'ere. Save it for a rainy windy night sat round the radiator.

'E called it The Two Robins, otherwise The Green Parrot, which became The Admiral Nelson, now a wallpaper ware'ouse.

Deelie   Your Uncle Robert is writin' a book about it.

Robert   A paper. It's called a paper. About the two illustrious gentlemen on a visit to our fair town.

Deelie   I thought it was a book?

Robert (*to* **David**)   I'm givin' a talk.

Deelie   Isn't it a book?

Robert   I 'ave to condense it before I can expand it! (*To* **David**.) For the Local History Society. (*To* **Aunt Deelie**.) Who've you bin tellin' it's a book?

Deelie   I've not told anybody.

Robert   So what 'ave you said, then?

Deelie   I've not said anything.

Robert   Nothin'?

Deelie   No.

Robert   A project your 'usband's researchin' and you've not let slip?

Deelie   No.

Robert   Well, I thought you might o' bin pleased to.

Deelie   You said it was secret. (*To* **David**.) It's his latest hobby.

Robert (*to* **David**)   It's a secret for the simple reason, dear boy, that yours truly has discovered some very revealing facts about said trip. Concerning a certain young lady.

Deelie   Robert.

Robert   You are looking at the very man whose detective work has unearthed a liaison for which the gentlemen's race-week perambulations were but a cover. Eh? Put it this way. Your Uncle Robert. Known and admired. Will be. National, never mind local literary circles. Sunday supplements . . .

Deelie   You'll have to take David to the library with you when you go.

Robert   Are you a member?

David   Yes.

Robert   I can be all day.

Pause.

Deelie   There or working out in 'is shed.

Robert   Out of bounds.

Deelie   That's to me and Charlene as well.

Robert   I've got it electrified.

Deelie   'E asn't.

Robert   That's where your Auntie got 'er permanent wave.

It's not exactly your dad's summer 'ouse, bein' as 'ow it's converted from a 'pigeon loft, but it'll do me.

So, will 'e manage to cope, do you think, with your mam in 'ospital and you with us? Or will it be too much for 'im?

Deelie   Robert! (*To* **David**.) You're not here to worry about any of that.

Robert   She's in the best place. They know what they're doin'. Your dad wouldn't 've put 'er there if it wasn't goin' to make 'er better. And 'e should know if anybody should. Shouldn't 'e?

David   I suppose so.

Robert   Change of scenery. Take your mind off.

And we're 'appy to 'ave you. Aren't we?

Deelie   Of course we are.

Robert   So. What's the plan for the morrow, dear boy?

David   Pardon?

Robert   What you goin' to be doin' with yourself?

David   I don't know.

Robert   Tour of the estate?

Deelie   Best not to wander too far.

Robert   What she means is, you the new kid on the block. Don't give 'em chance. Watch yourself. Gangs and what 'ave you. Few lunatics about.

Deelie   Must you?

Robert   Forewarned. If you come across a couple of la-las in long trousers, you'll know what I mean.

Deelie   He might want to sit in the garden and read.

Robert   Aye. Course. Glass o' barley water on the terrace. Ask nice and your Auntie Deelie'll tek for a tour of the grounds. Leisurely walk down past 'privet 'edge to the water feature.

Deelie   Take no notice.

Robert   'Drain outside 'back gate.

Deelie   It's not as if he's never been before.

Robert   I've landscaped it all since then.

I taught 'im 'ow to spit, didn't I?

Deelie   Robert –

Robert   Remember?

David   No.

Robert   Your dad loved that.

Charlene *comes in.*

Robert   Charlene'll show you round a bit, won't you?

Charlene   What?

Robert   Show 'im round. Your cousin David.

Charlene   No.

Robert   A bit of civility, please.

Charlene   What?

Deelie   She's got 'er own friends.

Robert   Aye, we know.

Charlene *moves through to the stairs.*

Robert   What you doin'?

Charlene   It's 'alf seven.

Robert   Upstairs to the boyfriend, is it?

Charlene   So?

Robert   I thought so.

Charlene *moves off.*

Robert   Give 'im my love.

Charlene   I will.

She is gone.

Deelie   I'll just take these up.

She takes up the backpack and suitcase, goes through.

Robert   Your dad wanted to give us lodge money. Finances unfortunately enterin' a difficult period – in short, we're a bit skint. But I said no. Something will turn up.

In fact, digging around Mr Dickens might well have already unearthed us a little nugget, eh?

You are our honoured guest, Master Davy.

Scene Two

Waste land. An abandoned, overgrown set of allotments. Sheds falling to pieces, nettles, brambles, bushes, bits of fencing, old rusting bits of bikes, burnt-out cars. A patch of flattened grass.

David *is mooching about.* **Wink** *appears, carrying a newspaper delivery bag – empty now. He watches* **David**, *then throws a stone at him.* **David** *looks round.*

Wink   What?

It weren't me.

It were some kid in a red jumper.

What you doin'?

David   Nothing.

Wink   This is private, all this. Don't you know that?

David   No.

Wink   Well, you do now.

What you lookin' for? You lost summat?

David   No.

Wink   Yeah, well, if you find it, it's mine. I lost some money down there. 'Ave you seen it?

David   No. I found a battery.

Wink   Is it dead?

David   I don't know.

Wink   'And it over.

David *gives him the battery.* **Wink** *licks it.*

Wink   Yeah, it is. It's mine.

He puts it in his pocket.

Where do you live?

David   I'm staying at my auntie's.

Wink   Where's she live?

David   Up there.

Wink   Which 'ouse?

David   Number twenty-seven.

Wink   *Daily Express.* Charlene's?

David   She's my cousin.

Wink   You livin' in 'er 'ouse?

David   Yes.

Wink   You got your own bedroom?

David   Yes.

Wink   Where you from?

David   Pardon?

Wink   Eh?

David   Pardon?

Wink   Where you from, I said.

David   The other side of town.

Wink   Where, exactly, as the crow flies?

David   Over there, I think.

Wink   Which is?

David   Sorry?

Wink   North? South? East? West?

David   I don't know.

Wink   Well, don't you think you should? What 'appens if you get lost?

David   I don't know.

Wink   Posh end, is it?

David   What?

Wink   You live in a posh 'ouse?

David   No.

Wink   Is it a prefab?

David   Pardon?

Wink   Like them over there?

David   No.

Wink   Posh, then, innit?

David   Not really.

Wink   You got any servants?

David   No.

Wink   You got a dad?

David   Yes.

Wink   'E's not dead, then?

David   No.

Wink   What does 'e do?

David   He's a doctor.

Wink   He's not, you liar.

David   He is.

Wink (*in some kind of odd American accent*)   Tell you what, sunshine, you wanna watch what comes out of your mouth. Somebody might fill it with a brick one of these days.

David   Pardon?

Wink   Fuckin' 'doctor'.

David   He is.

Wink   Yeah, well, my dad lives in Africa.

Gobbo *appears.*

Wink (*to* **David**)   This is 'is allotment. (*To* **Gobbo**.) Your allotment, innit?

Gobbo   What?

Wink   This. (*To* **David**.) You need our permission to come on 'ere.

David   I'm sorry.

Gobbo (*to* **Wink**)   What you doin'?

Wink   Just finished my papers. Where you bin?

Gobbo   Up the park. Who's this?

Wink   I think 'e's a spy.

David   I'm not.

Wink   You get tied up to a tree for spyin'.

David   I'm just standing here.

Wink   What's your real name, then?

David   David Moyle.

Wink   We could build a bonfire round a tree and then set light to it so 'e burns up.

David   I'm not doing anything. I didn't know it was yours.

Wink (*to* **Gobbo**)   That's what they did to you, innit, Gobbo?

Gobbo Not for spyin'. They just did it for summat to do.

David Can I go now, please?

Wink Where you goin'?

David Back to my auntie's.

Wink 'E's Charlene's cousin.

Gobbo 'E int.

Wink 'E is.

Gobbo You Charlene's cousin?

David Yes.

Wink 'E says 'is dad's a doctor an' all.

Gobbo 'E int.

Wink We can get you to tell the truth, you know.

David It is the truth.

Wink All we need is a knife. Mine's at 'ome.

Gobbo You ant got a knife.

Wink Yeah I 'ave.

Gobbo You ant.

Wink (*to* **David**) You got a knife?

David No.

Gobbo Penknife?

David I *am* Charlene's cousin. My dad *is* a doctor.

Wink He's scared.

Gobbo I think you'd better stop it, Wink.

Wink I'm only messin'.

Gobbo (*to* **David**) You're not cryin', are you?

David No.

Gobbo   Good.

I'm just off for a shit.

He goes off.

Wink   I could be an Indian tracker if I wanted to be.

You 'ave to read the signs. Animal tracks. Birds. How warm the horse shit, cold the ashes.

How long ago and how far away. How many there are, which way they went.

I was watching you ages. But you never knew I was there. I could've crept up on you and give you a rabbit punch before you knew what was 'appenin.

You can be in my commando club if you want.

David   No, thanks.

Wink   Don't you want to know how to fight?

David   No.

Wink   So what 'appens when there's a war?

David   What?

Wink   You 'ave to fight then, or they just come over and kill everybody, don't they?

David   I don't know.

Wink   Anyway, when a gang gets 'old of you, they *make* you fight.

David   I don't like fighting.

Wink   My dad was an SAS commando.

He was on a secret mission to blow up a nest of vipers.

David   Oh.

Wink   But 'e got captured and tortured and brainwashed so 'e never knew who 'e was any more, and 'e tried to escape and they shot him dead.

Only my grandma told me 'e wasn't dead, 'e'd managed to get away. It was another dead body what looked like 'im. 'E stowed away on a boat to Africa and 'e's still there, because 'e didn't know my mam was about to 'ave me. 'E lives in a mud 'ut and makes pots.

David   Oh.

Wink   It's true.

David   I never said it wasn't.

Wink   My grandma said Jesus showed 'er in a dream.

But nobody believed 'er, only me, so she got out of bed and went to fetch 'im.

David   Your grandma went to Africa?

Wink   She followed the railway lines. Only it was rainin' and she 'ad 'er 'ead bent down.

David   It ran her over?

Wink   I got my dad's will, and that. 'Is most prize possession. It's a book what 'e wrote what fits in a Swan Vestas, so you can pretend it's just matches.

'E wrote all this stuff in it so if 'e got stuck be'ind enemy lines, 'e could find 'is way back. Only 'e forgot to take it with 'im, that's why 'e got lost. It tells you about using the sun and your watch and that, to find your way.

It's my best thing. You're only allowed to see it if you join up.

Gobbo *returns.*

Gobbo   You got any paper?

Wink   Use dock leaves.

Gobbo   Not big enough. I'll 'ave to go 'ome, then.

Wink   Aren't we off up 'you-know-where'?

Gobbo   When?

Wink   Now?

Gobbo   I've just come back from there.

Wink   See owt?

Gobbo   Yes.

Wink   What, was that man there again, watchin'?

Gobbo   You bin tellin' 'im all about it?

Wink   No. I 'avent, 'ave I?

David   What?

Wink   I ant said 'owt. (*To* **David**.) Tell 'im.

David   I don't think he's told me.

Wink   I was tellin' 'im about my dad's book.

Gobbo   Our secret book?

Wink   I never said how you do it.

Gobbo   What you told 'im for? Is 'e in our club?

Wink   Do you want 'im to be?

Gobbo   Do you?

Wink   I don't know. (*To* **David**.) You got any binoculars?

David   No.

Wink   What '*ave* you got?

David   Nothin'.

Gobbo   You got any toilet paper?

David   No.

Wink   You got a tent?

David   No.

Wink   Torch?

David No.

Gobbo You've not got much, 'ave you?

David No.

Wink 'E's not livin' at 'ome, though, is 'e?

Gobbo Where's 'e livin'?

Wink Charlene's.

Gobbo 'E's not.

Wink 'E is, I told you. (*To* **David**.) You could go back 'ome and get it, though, couldn't you?

David What?

Wink You could nick somethin' from your proper 'ome for us.

David No.

Wink If you want to be in our club you 'ave to do what we say.

David I don't want to be in your club.

Wink Why not?

David I'd rather not, thank you.

Wink You get to be corporal.

David I don't want to be anything.

Wink You spying on us for another gang?

David No.

Wink We know stuff that other gangs would want to know, don't we?

Gobbo Why are you livin' at Charlene's?

David My mother's in hospital.

Wink   What's up wi' 'er?

David   I'm not sure exactly. I'm seeing her on Sunday.
I might find out then.

She'll be coming home soon.

Wink   Back to your posh 'ouse. Back to your dad the
doctor?

David   Yes.

Wink   You could nick some of them operating knives.
They'd be good.

Gobbo   'As she said anythin' about us?

David   Who?

Gobbo   About what we do sometimes with 'er?

Wink   Who? Charlene?

David   No. What?

Wink (*to* **Gobbo**)   Shurrup, then. Don't tell 'im.

Gobbo   I'm not. I'm findin' out if she 'as.

Wink   She ant.

Gobbo   I know.

Wink   You gonna nick us some operating knives, then?

David   Scalpels.

Gobbo   What do you want one of them for?

Wink   You could make dead sharp sticks. We're off to
make this trap, but we're not going to tell you where, are
we?

Gobbo   No.

Wink   We're off to dig this 'ole and put pointed sticks in it,
so this person we know will fall in it.

David   Who?

Wink   Yeah, as if we'd tell you. What? So you can tell 'im?

David   It's dangerous.

Wink   What d'you mean?

David   It could kill them.

Wink   Don't be stupid.

Gobbo   Could it?

David   Yes.

Gobbo   It'd only be little sticks.

Wink   In a little 'ole.

David   A dog could fall in it.

Gobbo   A cat couldn't, though. They're too clever for things like that. I've seen 'em.

Wink   They 'ant got a dog.

Gobbo   'E doesn't 'ave to 'ave, does 'e? It could be somebody else's.

I'm not doin' it now.

Wink   Yeah, but 'e called you a Gong Donkey.

Gobbo   I'm off to the toilet.

Scene Three

Aunt Deelie's *house.*

Charlene *is sitting at the table.* **Uncle Robert** *stands with his notes.*

Charlene   I'm missin' it!

Robert   Let 'im start without you.

Charlene   It's the omnibus edition.

Robert   'Grand Dramatic Company from London . . .'

Charlene   I've 'eard it.

Robert   I've rewritten it.

Charlene   Again?

Robert   Are you listenin'?

Charlene   No.

Robert   No. Not enough sex.

Charlene   What?

Robert   You'll 'ave to wait. I'm still sortin' that bit out.

Charlene   What you talkin' about?

Robert   'Im and 'is fancy piece.

Charlene   'Ow do you know what they did?

Robert   Well, I don't think they just 'eld 'ands and talked about books all night . . .

Deelie and **David** *come in.*

Charlene (*getting up*)   I'm upstairs.

Robert   'E gets run over tomorrow.

Charlene   Get lost.

Charlene *goes off.*

Robert (*to* **Aunt Deelie** *and* **David**)   She'd 'old a bloody wake for a week if he did.

'Ow was she?

Deelie   Not bad.

Robert   Oh? (*To* **David**.) Well, that's good then, innit?

Deelie *takes off her coat, sits beside* **David**.

Robert (*to* **Aunt Deelie**)   Can you lend me your ear 'oles in a minute?

Deelie   I'm tired.

Robert   The liaison. I'm workin' on it. Wants an audience. I'll fetch it through.

Deelie   Not now.

He goes off, back to his shed.

Deelie (*to* **David**)   There are bound to be things she won't remember. It's the treatment she's having. It'll come back. It'll all come back. She hasn't lost the last time you were home, she's just forgotten where she's put it.

It's not going to be long before she's back with us.

Trust me.

Out in that lovely big garden.

She loves her garden, doesn't she?

David   There's a man comes and does it all now.

Deelie   We're all here for her, all of us, aren't we? Lots of love to get her through it. Between us.

David   Sometimes I forget to think about her.

Deelie   You're allowed to.

David   It makes me not like myself much.

Deelie   She wants you to be happy.

She wouldn't want you like this.

David   We were happy. Before my dad sent me away.

Deelie   Your father only wants what's best for you.

Don't you like school?

David   She never wanted me to go.

Deelie   No. Wanted to hang on a bit longer. Before you became a young man. You grow up fast enough as it is.

Pause.

David   Wink and Gobbo really liked it at school.

Deelie   So did I.

David   Why aren't you there any more?

Deelie   Your Uncle Robert had just been finished on the railways and a job at the Spar shop came up, better money. I had to take it.

Still.

I see them out and about.

Robert *comes in, papers in hand.*

Robert   I don't want to be sued, see. I've got to make it subtle. I can't just say outright 'e were forty-five and knockin' off some eighteen-year-old piece using race week as a cover.

Deelie   Can we do this later?

Robert   It needs sortin'. I've nothin' concrete, see, but if 'e wasn't, it's a bloody coincidence the lass 'e finished up leavin' 'is missis for 'appened to be in town the very week –

Deelie   David, will you go and ask Charlene for my magazine?

Robert   What?

Deelie (*to* **Uncle Robert**)   I need to video something. I'm at work in an hour.

David *gets up.*

Deelie   Thank you.

David *goes off.*

Robert   What's that in aid of?

Deelie   I don't want that in front of the boy.

Robert   What?

Deelie   You know what

Robert   What, what 'appened with 'is mam and dad? Why not?

Deelie   I don't. All right?

Robert   'E never knew nowt about it.

Deelie   No. And I don't want him knowing this time.

Robert   Is 'is dad at it again? Same tart or a new one?

Deelie   It seems it never stopped.

Robert   The one from the 'ealth centre? 'Ow did you find out? Your Audrey?

Deelie   Yes.

Robert   So is this what's done it, then? Wrists and what 'ave you? Put 'er where she is? 'Ow did she find out?

Deelie   He was seen. Some 'friend' of Audrey's with the good sense to tell her.

Robert   You think the lad knows somethin'?

Deelie   He knows things aren't good. That's all. I don't want anything to suggest why.

Robert   So while your Audrey's in 'ospital, the good doctor –

Deelie   He wouldn't do that.

Robert   No? It's a perfect opportunity, int it?

Deelie   Stop it.

Robert   Dr Gregory Moyle. Eh? Upstanding pillar of the community.

Deelie   He's probably feeling very guilty about what's happened, right now.

Robert Oh, I bet 'e is. I mean, 'e's such a charmin', 'onourable man, in't he? It's all right, I've got the gist of 'is bedside manner.

Deelie Please . . .

Robert I might not 'ave a penny to scratch my arse, but I've never been the bloody 'eartache 'e is to 'is wife.

'Ave I?

I said –

Deelie No.

Robert That took some thinkin' about.

I'm good enough to look after 'is son while 'e swans off with some young tart, though. Did that occur to you?

Deelie He can't leave the boy on his own all day while he's at work. You know that's what it is.

Robert Or leave 'im at 'ome all night while 'e's givin' 'er a seein' to.

Deelie Stop it.

Robert Think about it.

Deelie I've no need to think about it. You're just talking filth now. I'm not listening.

Robert So will you listen to this?

'Grand Dramatic Company from London. Poses Plastiques in the Grand Assembly Room up the Stable Yard at seven and nine each evening. Grand Alliance Circus in the field beyond the bridge.'

'Now the bridge in question is The North Bridge, over what was then the newly-onstructed railway line. And the field, therefore, is Marshgate, until the nineteen thirties open land. Now lying somewhere between Dixon's Motors and the prison.'

David *returns.*

David   She said she gave it you back.

Declic   Did she? It'll be somewhere.

Robert   'Picture the scene, ladies and gentlemen. Our good friends the idle apprentices, Mr Dickens and Mr Collins, their first evening in town, out on a rising tide of humanity, making it's way along the Great North Road. A steam train billows its smoke around the parapets – '

I were thinkin' of puttin' in a bit there about tragic significance of steam trains to Dickens some years later. D'you think I should put summat in about 'railway plant works?

Deelie   If you like.

Robert   'E was in a very bad train accident, you know. And who was it who was accompanying 'im ? Well, it weren't Wilkie Collins. Make a note.

He does.

Right.

The sights and sounds of the circus appear. Quote: 'Grand Exhibition of Aztec Lilliputians, important to all who want to be horrified cheap. All for the Race Week.'

Deelie   I'll just do my programme.

She goes out.

Robert   Unquote. (*To **David***) All right?

David   Yes, thank you.

Scene Four

Waste land. **Charlene**, **David**, **Gobbo**, **Wink**.

David *sits watching* **Charlene** *and* **Gobbo**. **Wink** *stands very close to them, as director of the soap they are acting out. It's tense.* **Charlene** *is aggressive. As if they're expecting to get caught out, and have to be quick.*

Charlene   'Do you love me or don't you?'

Gobbo   'Yeah.'

Charlene   'Well then. Tell 'er tonight when you get 'ome for tea.'

Wink   After tea, or 'e won't get none.

Charlene (*to* **Wink**)   Just shut up, will you? (*To* **Gobbo**.) 'After tea.'

Wink (*prompting* **Gobbo**)   'What about the kids?'

Gobbo   Eh?

Wink   'What about the kids? I can't leave them.'

Gobbo (*to* **Charlene**)   'Yeah, what about the kids?'

Charlene   'What about me? They're all right. They don't need you. Not like I need you. You'll still get to see 'em, if you want, anyway.'

And you say, 'All right, I'll do it, then.'

Gobbo   'I'll do it, then.'

Charlene   'Tonight, we'll go away together.'

Gobbo   'Where we goin'?'

Charlene   'Anywhere'

Gobbo (*out of character*)   Can we go to Bridlington?

Charlene (*out of character*)   Eh? Yeah, whatever.

Gobbo   Brilliant. Yorkshire Belle and that.

Charlene   Will you just concentrate?

Gobbo   'I love you. Let's go to Bridlington in a caravan.'

Charlene   'We could stay in bed all day, if we wanted.'

Gobbo   'Yeah. If it's rainin'. Or we could go in the arcades.'

Charlene   'Take me now.'

Gobbo (*out of character*)   Aren't I supposed to be in my dinner break from the garage?

Charlene   'Take me upstairs, we've time.'

Gobbo   'What for?'

Charlene   'Take me upstairs. Come on. I want it.'

She starts to touch him. He's electrified, a rabbit caught in headlights. He can't move. She sees his distress. Stops, moves away.

Charlene   And cut. Scene Two. Action.

Wink *immediately takes on the role of* **Gobbo***'s wife. It's pantomime, like Old Mother Riley.*

Wink   'You bastard! I give you the best years of my life. I cook and clean for you, I wash the skid marks off your underpants, I go out to work, I come 'ome, I give you sex when you want it – not that you want it these days. I should have known somethin' was goin' on. How long 'ave you been seein' 'er?'

Gobbo   'Ages.'

Wink   'I suppose you were screwin' 'er while I was in 'ospital 'avin' my 'isterectomy?'

Gobbo   Eh?

Wink   'I 'ad my womb removed for you!'

Charlene   Yeah, all right.

Wink   'You two-timing bastard! Oh, dear God. Oh, no. What am I goin' to do?'

Gobbo   'Can I 'ave my suitcase?'

Wink   'I'll tell you what I'm goin' to do. Get your bloody self out of my 'ouse now!'

Gobbo   'Can I 'ave my –?'

Wink   You say, 'It's my 'ouse.'

Gobbo   'It's my 'ouse.'

Wink   'Oh no it isn't.'

Gobbo   'Oh yes it is.'

Wink   'I'll see you in court! You'll pay for this!'

Charlene   Yes, all right. That'll do. (*To* **David**.) Right, now you're my dad.

David *is embarrassed.*

Charlene   What?

Wink   Go on.

David   'You've been seeing somebody, haven't you?'

Charlene   No.

David   'What's this, then?'

Charlene   'A wristwatch. Where did you find that?'

Come on!

David   Do I have to?

Charlene   Just say it!

David   'Your mother found it in your bed.'

Charlene   'How did that get there?'

You say . . . 'You've been 'avin sex, or summat?'

David (*to* **Wink**)   You do it.

Wink   I'm 'is wife, I can't.

Charlene   Come on, come on! Do it!

David   'You've been having sex.'

Charlene (*instantly turning on him*)   'I'm sick of you accusin' me! I'm sick of it! You never did love me, did you? I'm leavin 'ome.'

And you say, 'Good riddance, you little slut.'

David   'Good riddance.'

Charlene   Say it all!

David   'Good riddance, you little slut!'

Charlene's *aggression turns to tears.*

Charlene   'I'm not stayin' where I'm not wanted.'

And I slam the door. Close-up on my face.

She is crying. They watch her, transfixed by the real tears. She suddenly snaps out of it.

And it's a wrap.

Thank you very much, everybody. Same time tomorrow.

David   I'm visiting my mother tomorrow.

Charlene   You'd better not go sayin' anythin' to anybody.

David   I won't.

Wink   Or we'll nail you to a plank.

Charlene *goes off.*

Wink   See you, Charlene.

Gobbo   See you, Charlene.

Are we off up the park?

Wink   I've got my paper round in a bit. I'm doing two rounds.

Gobbo   What for?

Wink   I'm savin' up for a pipe. And I need a new tea towel.

(*To* **David**.) Charlene says your mam's in the mental ward.

I've been in 'ospital loads of times. Not countin' visitin' my mam. I got a stick with a nail in it in my eye and it went like a slow puncture. 'E did it playing golf.

David   She's suffering from depression.

Wink   They do singing with tambourines.

David   No they don't.

Wink   They make plastic baskets.

David   I'm going.

Wink   You won't say owt, will you?

David   No.

Wink   We wouldn't really nail you to a plank.

Gobbo   'E got nailed to a plank one time, didn't you?

Wink   Yeah, but Charlene didn't do it. They did it at the woodyard where I used to sweep up. It didn't 'urt. They nail-gunned me through my coat sleeves and took me round the back and left me on a stack of pallets. They didn't take me off the plank till 'ome time. The bus driver wouldn't let me on the bus.

Gobbo   Why not?

Wink   Cause when I put my arms down they wanted to go back up again. (*He demonstrates.*) Jesus. I couldn't put my 'and in my pockets for my bus fare.

Gobbo *laughs and snorts. It sounds a bit like a donkey.*

David *chuckles.*

Wink   Me and Gobbo 'ad a committee meeting.

Gobbo   Did we?

Wink And we decided you don't need to pay us a subscription.

David I don't want to join.

Wink You 'ave to do a test instead.

Gobbo Like I did.

Wink You never did it.

Gobbo I did.

Wink When?

Gobbo When you weren't lookin.'

Wink You liar! (*To* **David**.) All right, tell you what, all you 'ave to do is swear on the book of finding your way when you're lost by my dad, that you'll keep all our club secrets . . .

David You haven't got any secrets.

Wink We've got 'undreds. We've got secrets about everybody. (*To* **Gobbo**.) Ant we?

Gobbo (*fed up*) Might 'ave.

Wink (*to* **David**) Even you.

David What?

Wink You're not a member. (*To* **Gobbo**.) Shall I tell 'im?

Gobbo You can if you like, I'm not bothered.

David What?

Wink You watched Charlene gettin' undressed one night.

David I didn't!

Wink She told us. She says you were sneakin' a look through the door.

David It's not true!

Wink She says she opened the door and you 'ad a bone on.

David   I didn't watch her. I didn't!

Wink   I know. I just made it up. I would.

Gobbo   You 'ave.

Wink   I know.

Gobbo   You could've been arrested.

Wink   She never 'ad no curtains one night. 'Window was open. I could hear this funny noise.

Gobbo   'E climbed up on their back wall with 'is 'ands down 'is trousers.

Wink   No, I didn't, then.

Gobbo   You did till 'er dad saw you.

Wink   They were decoratin'. 'E 'ad a squeaky paint-roller.

Is your bedroom next to 'ers?

David   Yes.

Wink   'Ow about a pair of 'er knickers?

David   No!

Wink   We'll let you be lieutenant colonel.

David   I don't want to be anything.

Wink   Well, if you don't want to join our society, we could join yours.

David   I haven't got one.

Wink   Well, invent one.

David   Like what?

Wink   We could 'ave adventures.

We could be finding mysteries to solve.

Detective investigations.

Gobbo   We're already doin' that.

Wink   Yeah, but we don't keep proper records. (*To* **David**.) You would be the one what like knew what was a real clue, and wrote it down in a book, with the time we found it. (*To* **Gobbo**.) We could do a different one every week.

Gobbo   So aren't we doin' mine any more, then?

Wink   What's that, then?

Gobbo   The man in the park.

Wink   He doesn't want to investigate that.

I could get some paper to make a notebook, and a pencil. You could write it so I've got an ID if I need to show it. And we could put down the times when we see suspicious things.

David (*to* **Gobbo**)   What does this man do?

Gobbo   He comes and watches when I'm Catcher in the Rye.

David   What?

Gobbo   He's a dark stranger. Are we doin' it?

Wink (*to* **David**)   That's 'is favourite book.

Gobbo   It might not be.

David   What's it about?

Wink   It's this boy who all he wants to do when 'e grows up is do this job where 'e's in this field full of all these little kids playing games and 'e 'as to make sure they stay in the field and don't go out of it and get lost or get hurt by people. So 'e keeps 'em safe.

That's what Gobbo's off to apply for. To be a Catcher in the Rye, innit?

Gobbo   I might.

Wink   'E looks after kids in the park, don't you?

Gobbo   Yeah. But the council don't pay me. I just do it for wanting to. And I don't 'ave a bell.

David   What's 'rye'?

Gobbo   It's the name of the field.

David   Why don't they just put a fence round it?

Gobbo   It wouldn't be a book then, would it? Anyway, they 'aven't got any money to build a fence. They did 'ave one, one time, but it was barbed wire and this boy got caught up on it and it went in 'is leg like a fish 'ook and they couldn't get it out, they 'ad to make a big 'ole in 'is leg and 'e screamed blue murder so 'is mother made 'em pull the fence down.

So what they did, they built a look-out tower in the middle of the field, and the catcher watches the little children all day, playing.

Wink   Can't 'e come down and play?

Gobbo   There's too many to watch. What 'e 'as to do, see, is when 'e sees one of the kids near the edge of the field, or 'e sees a dark stranger, 'e 'as to ring this bell, like a warning, so they stop, and then 'e comes down and fetches 'em back.

Wink   Like what the teacher used to do at playtime to get everybody lined up.

Gobbo   Yeah.

Wink   Is it a big field?

Gobbo   Massive. And there's all tall corn waving in the wind in the other fields all round, higher than the little ones can see over, so they would get lost and never find their way out. And at the edge of these fields big cliffs what go a long way down. And anyway, there's combined harvesters.

Wink   Does 'e 'ave any binoculars?

Scene Five

Aunt Deelie's *house*. **Uncle Robert**, **Charlene**, **David**.

Robert   The town were teeming, heavin' wi' folk. No
room at the inn. Everywhere full. Not a one. So the doctor's
tryin' all these places, 'e's getting' further and further out o'
town, and times gettin' on. 'E's walked miles, it's close on
midnight, when 'e comes to this run-down old coachin' inn.
Sign creakin' in the wind. The Two Robins. Dark and
dismal place. As 'e's goin' in, there's this bloke comin' out,
followed by the landlord. The bloke says, 'No chance, mate,
I wouldn't sleep there if you paid me,' and scurries off into
the night. 'Any rooms?' asks 'doctor. 'Aye,' says landlord.
'One just unexpectedly come up. If you don't mind spendin'
a night in the same room as a dead body. Gentleman died
on me this evening.'

Well, there's nothin' for it but to tek it, bein' as 'ow 'e's in
the middle o' nowhere, middle o' the night.

Charlene   Did this really 'appen?

Robert   It's a ghost story, if you'll let me tell it. 'E got the
idea while 'e's wanderin' 'streets while Dickens were
otherwise.

Charlene   Otherwise what?

Robert   So. 'Landlord lights 'candle, teks 'im up all these
stairs, till they come to this room. Opens 'door and there's
body, laid out under sheet in 'four poster bed. Landlord
points to a single bed in the corner. Doctor thanks 'im, teks
'candle, creaks across floorboards and gets himself sorted for
the night. 'E keeps candle lit, like, doesn't want to be in the
pitch black, but course 'e can't sleep, 'e's one eye on the
clock, other on 'corpse, when it suddenly moves, sits up.

Charlene   It's not dead, then?

Robert   Eh? No.

Charlene   So it's not a ghost, then?

Robert   What?

Charlene   'Ow is it a ghost story?

Robert   You do it deliberate, don't you?

Charlene   What?

Robert   Do you want to 'ear it or don't you?

Charlene   No, not particularly.

Robert   That tele's comin' out of your room.

Charlene   What 'ave I done now?

Robert   You're a mardy-arsed little sod. If your programme doesn't go the way you want it to, we get the consequences. It's a soap. 'E's not a real person. All right?

Charlene   I know that. I'm not stupid.

Robert   'E teks up with some tart, and we can't talk to you for a week.

Charlene   You have your stories . . .

Robert   Look, what I am dealing with is fact. What you sit and drool over is fiction. If you can't tell the difference –

Charlene   You got proof now, then?

Robert   What?

Charlene   You got proof it 'appened? You said you didn't 'ave, so it's not fact, it's what you think *might* 'ave appened.

Robert   'E finished up buyin' 'er an 'ouse to live in, the same lass, if that doesn't tell you somethin'. Can we get back to –

Charlene   But nobody ever actually caught 'em doin' anythin'.

Robert   Don't come it, just because we've company. What I *do* know is, as is reported, 'Dickens and Collins left for London in a hurry, in circumstances not explained.'

Charlene   So they did get caught?

Robert   I 'ave to be careful what I say.

Charlene   Why?

Robert   Are we listenin' to this ghost story, or what?

Charlene   Or what?

Robert   I'm tryin' to bring a bit of culture to the proceedin's!

Family sat round. It's oral 'istory, innit? Talk about the lost art of storytellin'. It's lost and gone forever in this 'ouse.

You might learn summat.

Charlene   I 'ave. It's borin'.

Robert   There's no 'ope for you, lass.

Charlene   Yeah, I know, you told me.

Robert   What was the last book you read?

Charlene   What?

Robert   If you bothered to read summat other than agony aunts an' 'oroscopes, you might start –

Charlene   What, like 'im?

Robert   Yes, like 'im. 'E's a damn sight more –

Charlene   I'll tell you why 'e spends all 'is time readin'.

Robert   Why?

Charlene   What friends 'ave you got, David?

David   I've got friends round here.

Charlene *knows who he means, is suddenly scared.*

Robert   Who? Round 'ere?

David   Yes.

Robert   Who?

Charlene *moves away.*

David   Gobbo says to tell you he's not leaving his wife.

Charlene *stops, turns to him.*

Robert   The Gong Donkey? (*To* **Charlene**.) What's that supposed to mean?

Charlene   I don't know, do I?

Robert (*to* **David**)   'As 'e been 'angin round talkin' to you? What's 'e said?

David   Nothing. He just said he knew Charlene.

Robert   'Leavin' 'is wife'?

David (*backing down*)   It might have been something else he said.

Deelie *comes in, in her Spar uniform.*

Robert   He's an idiot.

Charlene   He's not an idiot.

Robert (*to* **David**)   He'd 'ang on your Auntie Deelie's skirts all playtime. An' I'm talkin' at twelve year old, not two. *And* she'd let 'im.

Deelie   What?

Robert   Maybe not such an idiot, eh? Gettin' a grope.

Deelie   What are you talking about?

Robert   Was the other one with 'im?

David   Yes.

Robert   'E would be. Watch yourself. (*To* **Charlene**.) And you. Be warned, the pair of you.

Charlene   I've not done anythin'. I don't know what 'e's on about. What would I want to 'ang about wi' them for?

Robert   I'm just tellin' you.

Charlene Yeah. I know. I 'eard you.

David What's a 'Gong Donkey'?

Robert Courtesy of Mr Dickens. Describin' a ravin'
drunken lunatic staggerin' about our fair town, who kept
makin' 'orrible noises somewhere between a gong and the
brayin' of an ass.

Deelie The police are all over the park. Some little girl's
gone missing.

Scene Six

Waste land. **Charlene**, **David**, **Wink**, **Gobbo**. *They are acting
out a scene.* **Wink** *is holding on to a rusty corrugated sheet, which
becomes his 'cupboard'.*

Wink (*to* **Gobbo**) 'If you think I'm goin' to spend the
night in the broom cupboard, Dickens, just so you can
entertain your young lady.'

Charlene (*to* **Gobbo**) And you say, 'But you promised to
find another room'

Gobbo 'But you promised to find another room.'

Wink 'There int any other rooms! They've all bin taken.'

Charlene (*to* **Gobbo**) And you say, 'So take the broom
cupboard.'

Gobbo 'So take the broom cupboard.'

Charlene *knocks at the imaginary door.*

Wink 'She's here. Bugger it. I suppose I shall 'ave to
spend the night in the broom cupboard.'

Charlene Wink?

Wink What?

Charlene Wilkie Collins wouldn't say 'Bugger it.'

Wink   So's 'I'm a bit upset at this, Dickens. It'll cost you a fiver.'

Charlene   Yeah. Good. (*To* **Gobbo**.) And you say, 'Oh, very well, a fiver it is.'

Gobbo   What do I 'ave to give 'im a fiver for?

Wink   To shut me up, so I don't say nowt.

Gobbo   'Here.'

He pretends to hand him a fiver.

Wink   'Right.' And then I go and open the cupboard, get inside and lay down.

He does this. Sits up.

'I hope, Dickens, that you won't make a row shaggin' 'er and keep me awake.'

Gobbo   No.

Charlene   You say, 'I wouldn't dream of it.'

Gobbo   'I wouldn't dream of it.'

Wink *lays down.*

Charlene *knocks on the door again.* **Gobbo** *opens it.*

Gobbo   'Eh up.'

Charlene   'Oh, my dearest Dickens. A terrible time I had in getting here.'

Gobbo   ''Ow come?'

Charlene   'The streets of Doncaster are full of drunks and villains. Still, I am here, my love.'

Gobbo   'You'd best come in, then.'

Charlene *steps into the room. The 'door' is closed.*

Charlene   And I undo my bonnet and you take my shawl off.

Gobbo   Your 'what' off?

Charlene   My shawl. Off my shoulders.

He does.

'Do you love me?'

Gobbo   'Yeah.'

Charlene   'Really? How much?'

Gobbo   'A lot.'

Charlene   'More than the sun, the moon, the stars?'

Gobbo   'Yeah.'

Charlene   Say it, then.

Gobbo   'I love you more than the sun, the moon, the stars.'

Charlene   'Oh Charles, you have such a way with words.'

She laughs loudly and then points at **David**, *who 'knocks' on the door.*

Charlene   'Oh no, the landlord. Quick. Hide me. In the broom cupboard.' And you say, 'No, not in there.'

Gobbo   'No, not in there,'

Charlene   'Why not?'

Gobbo   'It's full of . . .' I forgot.

Wink   Brooms, you dingbat!

Charlene   'Quick. I'll hide behind the door. Don't let him in.'

David *'knocks' again.* **Gobbo** *opens the door.*

David   'Excuse me, Mr Dickens, sir, but I thought I heard a noise. A sort of giggle. Like a lady.'

Gobbo   'No. No lady in 'ere, landlord.'

David   'I'm very sorry to have troubled you.'

Gobbo   'That's all right.'

Gobbo *shuts the 'door'.*

Charlene   And then you hold me in your arms.

Gobbo *takes her in his arms.*

Charlene   And then you kiss me.

Gobbo   Can't somebody else?

Wink   I suppose I'll 'ave to do it.

Charlene   Shut up.

She kisses **Gobbo** *quickly on the cheek.*

Charlene   All right, Scene Two.

It's two o'clock in the mornin', and we're in bed, right.

Wink   'Avin a fag, after.

Charlene   Asleep.

They lie down together.

Charlene *sits up.*

And then I wake up wantin' a wee. And I can't find the po, so I need to go to the loo.

She gets up.

'Oh dear. It's very dark. Perhaps if I can find a candle . . .'

And I light this candle and I go over to what I think is the door out, an' I open it . . .

She 'opens' the 'broom-cupboard door'.

And I see what I think is a dead body.

She screams. **Gobbo** *gets up,* **Wink** *gets up, hands over his ears.*

Wink   Chuffin' ell!

Charlene   Come on!

Wink   'My dear lady, you look as if you'd seen a ghost. I'm not dead. I'm just sleepin' 'ere. Shurrup, then, you'll wake everybody up. Dickens, I can't seem to shut 'er up. Shall I give 'er a slap?'

Charlene   You dare.

David *knocks on the 'door'.*

David   'What's goin' on in there?'

Wink   'It's the landlord.'

David   'Hello? Mr Dickens?'

Charlene   An' I start to pass out with the shock.

She drops into **Gobbo***'s arms.* **Robert** *appears. Stops, watches unseen.*

Gobbo   What do I do?

David   'Mr Dickens? I'm coming in.'

Wink   'Put 'er under the bed!'

He grabs **Charlene***'s legs. They walk her to the 'bed'.* **David** *comes in.* **Uncle Robert** *walks over to them.* **Wink** *and* **Gobbo** *see him, drop* **Charlene***.* **David***, oblivious, carries on.*

David   'What's going on? What's a woman doing in here? What do you two think you are doing with that young lady? Pick her up and get out of my hotel, the lot of you!'

He turns, sees **Uncle Robert***.* **Charlene** *sees him, gets up.*

Robert   I 'eard somebody scream.

Charlene   I'm all right.

Robert (*to* **Gobbo**)   What were you doin'?

Charlene   Nothin'.

Robert   I'm talkin' to 'im.

Gobbo   We were doin' a play.

Charlene made it up for us.

Wink   Shut it, Gobbo.

Robert (*to* **Wink**)   And what's it about?

Charlene   We're just messin' about.

Robert   I asked him, not you.

(*To* **Gobbo**.) What were you doin' with 'er?

Charlene   'E weren't doing anythin'.

Robert (*still to* **Gobbo**)   Eh?

Gobbo   I was bein' Charles Dickens.

Robert *smacks him across the face.* **Gobbo** *takes it, doesn't react, just keeps looking at him.* **Uncle Robert** *turns to* **Charlene**.

Robert   I 'eard somebody scream. I thought – with that little lass missin' –

Charlene   It was my idea, not theirs.

Robert   Get off 'ome!

Charlene *stands her ground.*

Robert   Now. Move.

Charlene *goes off.*

Robert   (*to* **Wink**) You think it's a joke, do you?

Wink   Erm . . . Yeah?

Uncle Robert *makes a move for him.*

Wink   I mean no.

Uncle Robert *stops. He turns to* **David**. *Disappointed.* **David** *can't look at him.*

Robert   The landlord of the Angel Hotel.

Thank you, David. Thank you very much.

(*To* **Gobbo**.) You ever touch 'er . . . You put your 'ands on 'er again . . . I'll kill you.

He turns, goes off.

Wink   I only 'ad one line left to say.

(*To* **Gobbo**.) 'Tell you what, Dickens, this gives me a great idea for a ghost story.'

Gobbo   Might she really scream?

Wink   Who?

Gobbo   The little girl?

Scene Seven

Aunt Deelie's *house.* **Aunt Deelie**, **Uncle Robert**, **Charlene**, **David**.

Robert   Prince Monolulu.

Deelie   Who?

Robert   Prince Monolulu.

Deelie   The one that used to dress up as a Zulu?

Robert (*with derision*)   Zulu.

Deelie   He did, didn't he?

Robert   He was an 'onolulu prince, you daft get!

Deelie   I thought he was a Zulu.

Robert   What, in a bloody grass skirt? Flowers round 'is neck?

(*To* **David**.) He'd walk round town in all his regalia shouting 'I got a horse! I got a horse! And it's goin' to win!' Tipster. What you call a colourful character.

Charlene   And did it?

Robert   What?

Charlene   Win?

Robert (*to* **David**)   When I were your age, it were what you *call* an event, not like now. Town'd be packed. Heavin'. You couldn't move for folk from all over. Wonderful sight.

David   I saw some gypsy caravans this morning.

Deelie   They come for the races.

David   On the main road.

Charlene   There's some up the back of the railway.

Robert   What, over yon?

Charlene   They've been there days.

Robert   Best get another bloody lock put on the shed, then. No end broke into last year. You can't leave nowt lyin' about. They whip owt if they think they can flog it. And you watch yourself.

Charlene   What do you mean?

Robert   You know what I mean. 'Angin' about.

Charlene   Does that mean I'm not grounded any more?

Robert   It means you do as you're bloody well told. You don't 'ang about wi' no undesirables. That pair of weirdos *or* your baked 'edge'og brigade.

Deelie   It's nice to see race week popular again, isn't it?

Robert *looks at her with scorn.*

Robert   Nothin' to do wi' 'orse racin' nowadays, is it? It's all about – what is it? – 'corporate 'ospitality suites'? Salmon and champagne and sales reps entertainin' 'alf-cut clients in tents. 'Ladies' day?' You see 'em, great fat pieces fallin' legless out o' limousines. That's before they've even got to the bloody enclosure. They wouldn't know a winner from a seaside donkey.

Deelie (*to* **David**)   Your Grandad always had a bet on the St Leger. Your grandma too. She used to dream hers the night before. We got an ice cream if it won.

Charlene   So who was he then, this St Leger? Did he look after horses like the other one?

Robert   What?

Charlene   The one with the birds and that –

Deelie   St Francis, you mean?

Charlene   Yes.

Robert   Lord St Leger. It was a *Lord* St Leger, you pair of planks. 'E 'ad a wager wi' another bloke. 'My horse can outrun your horse, old chap.' So the other bloke bet 'im it couldn't and that were the start of it. Seventeen hundred and sixty-eight.

Deelie   So it would've been well under way by Dickens's day, then?

Robert   Of course it was. It were practically 'Wimbledon of 'sports calendar by then.

Deelie (*to* **David**)   He's finished his paper. Sent off a copy to the Local History Society.

Robert   First draft. It's called the first draft. They like to know what your talk's gonna be about. See if you might need any visual aids, and such.

Deelie   A week on Saturday.

Robert   Falls in with race week, see. A few big wigs there. Industry bosses. Councillors.

Deelie   I'd be terrified.

Robert   We've all got the same intellectual curiosity.

Charlene   'Ow do you know? You've never been before.

Robert   I was invited because of my particular area of expertise.

Charlene   You asked David's dad if 'e could put a word in.

Robert   Don't come it. He suggested it. I can extend your telly ban another week if you want.

Charlene   Not bothered.

Robert   No, course you're not.

Charlene   I'm not. If you must know, you've done me a favour and weaned me off.

Robert   That'll be the day.

You can miss six month and still pick up where you left off.

Charlene   Yeah, course you can.

Robert   Do they think that's 'ow we live? In and out of one another's ouses, in the pub, in the café, pokin' our noses into other folks's business, 'avin affairs left, right and centre? They must do. You do.

Charlene   I don't.

Robert   Your 'eads nowt but bloody soap suds.

Charlene   Yeah, right.

Robert   Well, there's bugger-all else goes on in there.

Charlene *gets up, about to move off.*

Robert   When are you goin' to take an interest in anythin' worthwhile?

Deelie   Don't, Robert, please. We've had all this.

Robert   She's eighteen!

Deelie   She's on a college course, isn't she?

Robert She's switched twice to *my* knowledge. 'Air and Beauty! I were two year into a railway engineerin' apprenticeship at 'er age.

Charlene Yeah, and look where it got you.

Robert What?

Deelie Don't, Charlene.

Robert What's that mean?

Deelie She doesn't mean anything.

Robert I were made redundant, weren't I?

Charlene Were you? I never knew that.

Robert I still manage to put a bloody roof over your 'ead, though, don't I?

Charlene I thought your dole did that. What, you mean deliverin' pizzas? I thought that were your beer money?

Deelie Stop it, the pair of you! Stop it!

Robert Maybe I should've gone in for medicine so we could all be playin' 'appy families.

Aunt Deelie *gets up, makes to go through to the kitchen.*

Robert (*to* **Aunt Deelie**) You making tea?

She stops. **David** *watches her.*

Robert (*to* **Charlene**) You won't always 'ave me and your mother to run round after you, you know.

Charlene You?

Robert You know what I mean. I mean when you finally decide to set up on your own. Or is the boyfriend meant to provide? If you ever get a real one.

Charlene What, you want me out?

Deelie He's not sayin' that.

Charlene   What's 'e sayin', then?

Robert   You'll find out 'ow 'ard it really is then. When you 'ave council tax and what-'ave-you, bills at the end of every month. Only ones get out of that are these lot over the back. Gold teeth and Capo di Monte in their caravans and don't pay a bloody penny.

David   Somebody said it was gypsies that took the little girl.

Deelie   Who?

David   Some women in a shop.

Deelie   It's not gypsies.

Robert   It's somebody she knows.

Deelie   How do you know?

Robert   I'm tellin' you. They taught about it enough in your school – 'Don't talk to strangers.' Somebody she trusted.

Deelie   Do you think?

Robert   Maybe the Gong Donkey knows more about it than 'e's lettin' on.

Deelie   What?

Charlene   What are you sayin'?

Robert   It's not me. Just what some folk are sayin'.

Deelie   Who?

Charlene   What are they sayin'?

Robert   I'm sayin' nowt.

Deelie   No. Don't you ever!

Robert   What?

Deelie   Don't you ever say anything against that boy. Do you hear me?

Robert   I thought 'e were a man. You 'eard it said an' all, then, 'ave you?

Scene Eight

Waste land. **Wink**, **Gobbo**, **David**.

Wink, *smoking his new pipe, is interrogating* **Gobbo**, *who is kneeling on the floor, hands tied behind his back, blindfolded. He's scared. It's a game, but it's deadly serious.* **David** *stands watching, carrying a half-drunk carton of Ribena.*

Gobbo   Hello? Hello? Are you there? Wink? What you doin?

Wink   So where was you that afternoon?

Gobbo   I've told you, I can't remember.

Wink   Not good enough.

Gobbo   It wasn't me. Look, can we stop now?

Wink   Shut your mouth. I'll ask the questions. You know you did it. Why don't you just tell me where she is, then we can all go 'ome?

Gobbo   I don't know, I don't know.

David   I think you should stop now.

Wink   Look, I'm intelligence. You're caterin'. All right?

He takes the carton from **David**.

Wink (*to* **Gobbo**)   What was she wearing?

Gobbo   A blue dress and sandles.

Wink   'Ow do you know?

Gobbo   The picture in the paper.

Wink   You know because you took 'er!

Gobbo   I never. I never.

Wink   You went to the park . . .

Gobbo   No.

Wink   You gave 'er some sweets.

Gobbo   I didn't!

Wink   You took 'er by the 'and and led 'er away and you've put 'er somewhere.

Gobbo   No.

Wink   You've 'idden 'er away. Chained 'er up so she can't escape.

Gobbo   I would never *do* that.

Wink   You put a gag round 'er mouth so she can't scream.

Gobbo   Please don't say these things. I get pictures.

Wink   What pictures?

Gobbo   Dungeon pictures.

Wink   Is that where she is?

Gobbo   It might be.

Wink   What do you mean, 'It might be'?

Gobbo   In a cellar somewhere.

Wink   You put 'er in a cellar?

Gobbo   No. But that's where she might be. If I look in my mind that's what I can see. She's cryin' and dirty and I don't like it. Because it's my fault. I should 'ave taken care of 'er and I never.

Wink *tries another tactic. Softly softly.*

Wink   All right. All right, Gobbo. I'm sorry.

Gobbo   Can I go now?

Wink *gets close to* **Gobbo**, *takes a noisy slurp from the carton.*

Wink   I expect you want a drink.

Gobbo   Yes please.

Wink   What would you like?

Gobbo   Can I 'ave a sip of your Ribena?

Wink *bends down close to* **Gobbo***'s head, rattles up the last dregs of Ribena through the straw.*

Wink   Oh dear. Just finished it.

What does she drink?

Gobbo   Who?

Wink   Your friend?

Gobbo   I 'aven't given 'er a drink.

Wink   She's goin' to die of thirst, you bastard!

Gobbo   I never! I never!

David   Stop it, now. He's had enough. I'm not doing this now.

Wink (*to* **David**)   All right, untie 'im.

David *moves towards* **Gobbo**.

Gobbo   Can I go?

Wink   No. I just want your 'ands so I can put splinters down your nails.

Gobbo   Get lost!

Wink *stops* **David**.

Wink   Don't you tell me to get lost, sonny boy. I'll 'ave you, sunshine, I'll 'ave you.

Gobbo   I don't want to play this any more.

Wink   We all want to go 'ome, lad. My wife's forgotten what I look like.

Gobbo   You're not doin' it properly.

Wink   Aren't I?

Gobbo   They don't put splinters down your nails.

Wink   Oh, don't they? Who says? This isn't telly, you know.

Gobbo   I know.

Wink   Confess, then!

Gobbo   No.

Wink (*to* **David**)   All right, get the drill.

Gobbo   What drill?

David   I'm not doing this.

Silence.

Gobbo   Wink? Wink?

He starts to sing a tune to himself. It's 'Little Donkey'.

Little Donkey, little donkey,
On the dusty road.
Little donkey, little donkey,
With your heavy load . . .

Wink   All right, switch on.

Gobbo   All right, I did it!

Wink   I knew it.

Gobbo   I did it!

Wink (*to* **David**)   All right, untie 'im. Take the blindfold off.

David *does this. We see now that* **Gobbo** *has a bruised face. He stands, rubbing his legs.*

Wink *is upset now, almost crying* .

Wink   You're goin' to get put away.

Gobbo   I'm not, am I? Wink? I'm not, am I?

David   No. (*To* **Wink**.) Don't tell him that. Obviously the police don't suspect him or they would've come for him by now, with all that's being said.

Wink   No shit, Sherlock.

Gobbo   They 'ave to suspect the man we saw. We need to 'and our time-sheets in to the police.

Wink   What for?

Gobbo   I told you before, but you wouldn't listen!

Wink   So? If we tell them what he looked like and show them all the times we saw him, then what?

Gobbo   It might help the police solve the mystery.

Wink   They won't buy it.

David   They might.

Gobbo   Your dad's a doctor. They'd believe you.

Wink   Look –

Gobbo   Would you dare?

David   I don't know.

Wink (*to* **Gobbo**)   You're still a prisoner. I 'aven't finished with you.

Gobbo   You could write down what 'e looks like and post it through the letter box.

David   Description.

Gobbo   It'd be anonnymans tip off.

Wink   Look. Shut it. You're still in debriefin'.

David (*to* **Gobbo**)   You mean we don't put our names on it? I don't think they would accept that.

Gobbo   You've got to show it to Charlene's mum, then. Tell 'er all about it. Ask 'er to put 'er name on it. Will you?

David   I'll ask her about it.

Wink (*to* **David**)   It doesn't matter if you take it to the police, does it? Till they find where the girl is, 'e's one of them escaped goats what everybody chases after, int 'e?

Gobbo   A what?

Wink   We just get sick of getting' smacked in all the time. 'E's my best friend in the whole world and I just need to make 'im more sensible!

(*To* **Gobbo**.) You've got to be ready.

Gobbo   I am ready. I've said some prayers. And I'm not comin' out to play evenin's and weekends.

Wink   He's just gonna say what anybody wants 'im to say. I know 'e is.

Gobbo   My knees were 'urtin'.

Wink   They'll 'urt when they kneecap you.

Gobbo   Police don't do that.

Wink   Well, what about when some gang gets 'old of you? Eh? What then?

Gobbo   They'll chuck a brick at me, shout Gobbo, and I'll turn round and it'll go bam in my face like last time.

Wink   No. They'll grab 'old of you.

Gobbo   They'll grab 'old of me.

Wink   And punch you in the face.

Gobbo   Punch me in the face.

Wink   With knuckledusters.

Gobbo   They won't, will they?

Wink   They'll kick you down.

Gobbo   On the floor.

Wink   Right.

Gobbo   They'll push my 'ead in a bucket of water.

Wink   Gobbo. You're my best friend, aren't you?

Gobbo   Yeah.

Wink   If you give in, and start sayin' stuff you never did, they could put you in an 'ole and throw stones at you till you're dead.

Gobbo *is crying now.*

Wink   You think I want to do this?

It's a job. It's what I'm trained to do.

David   When?

Wink   What do you mean, 'when'?

David   Were you in the army?

Wink   Secret trainin'.

David   I don't believe you.

Wink   My dad taught me.

David   You've never seen your dad.

Wink   Yes I 'ave, then.

David   When?

Wink   Look. If you must know, it came in my brain while 'e was bein' tortured and I was bein' born. All right?

Gobbo   Can I borrow your dad's Swan Vestas book?

Wink   What for?

What, you runnin' away?

Gobbo   If I know where I am, I won't get lost.

Wink   You can't run away.

Gobbo   Why not?

Wink   They'll think you're guilty, won't they?

Gobbo   They do anyway.

Wink   You're not runnin' away!

Gobbo   If they get me, will you make sure you tell my nanna I never did it?

Wink   Yes.

Gobbo (*to* **David**)   Will you tell Charlene's mum I never did it as well?

David   She knows that.

Gobbo   Does she? Really?

David   Yes.

Gobbo   She was my favourite teacher.

My nanna's got no money for a proper coffin. She told me. I'll 'ave to go in a cardboard box.

Wink   Oh chuff.

Gobbo   What?

Wink   I've 'ad an idea.

Gobbo   You ant.

Wink   Chuffin' 'ave.

Gobbo   What?

Wink   Elementary, innit, Watson? We build a proper hide-out. Underground. We nick a spade and dig a dug-out what nobody can see. It'd be a dead good den. Nobody would know where it is, 'ceptin us. Like what Vietcong 'ad.
A tunnel leadin' to it. Entrance all covered up. An' we bring 'im food an' that.

Gobbo   What, I sleep there?

Wink   Yeah. There was this man on telly, right, and 'e tried to get in *The Guinness Book of Records* only they wouldn't let 'im because they said 'e was mad. 'E ad this underground coffin in a pub yard and they 'ad these tubes to feed 'im and a tube to the beer barrel, and 'e' stayed right through Christmas and came out New Year.

Gobbo   'Ow did 'e go to the toilet?

Wink   Eh? Well 'e 'ad some more tubes an' that. And a funnel.

Gobbo   I'm not shittin' down a funnel in a coffin.

Wink   You don't 'ave to, do you? You come out at night.

Gobbo   Like a badger.

Wink   Yeah.

Gobbo   Like a fox.

Wink   Yeah, like a fox.

Gobbo   Hedgehog.

Wink   Yeah, all right! We get the idea.

Look, we're doin' it, right?

Gobbo   Really?

Wink   Yeah.

Gobbo   Yeah.

Wink *looks to* **David**.

David (*unconvinced*)   Yeah.

Wink   It'll be brilliant!

Gobbo   Yo!

Wink (*American army route-march chant*)   We are going to build a den!

Gobbo *responds. Together they do a little dance.*

Gobbo We are going to build a den!

Wink You won't ever find us then!

Gobbo You won't ever find us then!

Scene Nine

Aunt Deelie's *house.*

Uncle Robert, *before his 'audience',* **David** *and* **Charlene**. **Charlene** *looks at* **David**, *who dare not meet her eyes.*

Robert And Mr Dickens continues, quote: 'The dearest friend the Gong Donkey has in all the world is a sort of Jackall, in a dull, mangy, black hide. Drunk too, he advances at the Gong Donkey, with a hand on each thigh, in a series of springs and stops, wagging his head as he comes. The Gong Donkey –

Charlene *catches the eye of* **David**. *She mouths 'Where is he?'* **David** *shrugs, shakes his head.*

Robert regarding him with attention and with the warmest affection, suddenly perceives that this is the greatest enemy he has in the world, and hits him hard in the countenance. The astonished Jackall closes with the Donkey, and they roll over and over in the mud, pummelling one another. A Police Inspector, supernaturally endowed with patience, who has long been looking on from the Guildhall steps, says, to a myrmidon, "Lock 'em up! Bring 'em in!"' '

He looks up, smiling. **Charlene** *beams back.*

Robert The Guildhall, of course, was on the site of our present Marks and Spencer's.

Charlene Fascinatin' stuff, innit?

And **Uncle Robert** *returns to his script.*

Robert This next bit is me, not Dickens.

I've a page missin'. Stop the clock.

He looks at his watch.

'Ow long so far?

Charlene   An hour?

Robert   Seven minutes.

He looks at the rest of the script, flipping over the pages, looking for the missing one.

Crowds at the races . . . last night at the Angel Hotel . . . departure from station on train to London. Dickens writes up notes for *Household Words* . . . Collins begins his ghost story.

Deelie *comes in.*

Charlene (*getting up*)   Right, break out the vollyvons.

(*To* **Aunt Deelie**.) Cup of tea?

Deelie   I'd love one.

Charlene *goes into the kitchen.*

Robert (*getting up*)   You finally got 'ere, then?

Deelie   I waited ages for a bus. Traffic in town.

Robert   I told you what it'd be like, midweek.

Deelie   Your mother's doing well. They're very pleased with her.

Robert   I'm a page missin'.

He goes out.

Deelie   Very pleased.

David   Did you hand it in?

Deelie   I've been to the hospital.

David   You said you would.

Deelie   I said I would think about it. I can't just walk in to a police station with a notebook.

David   Why not?

Deelie   Because. They would want to see the three of you for a start.

David   So we'll tell them where he is and they can come and fetch him and interview him.

Deelie   He wouldn't know what to say.

David   You be there.

Deelie   Look, it doesn't matter what I think about it. Once they see who's written it, nobody is going to –

David   You never even took it with you, did you?

Deelie   David . . .

David *makes to go out.*

Deelie   David! Don't you want to hear about your mother?

He stops. **Charlene** *comes in.*

Deelie   Just wait a minute.

David   You said she was all right.

Deelie   She is. They've told her if she carries on making the progress she is doing, they might let her out for the weekend. That'll be nice, won't it?

David   Yes. It will.

He makes to go out.

Charlene   Where you going? Wait.

David *is gone.*

Pause. **Charlene** *turns to* **Aunt Deelie***.*

Charlene   She's going home, then?

Deelie   She got a bit excited when they told her, but they managed to calm her down. They've got 'er on some different medication now. Seems to be doing the trick.

Charlene   That's good. That's great. What's he being funny about it for?

Deelie   I don't think he wants to believe it till it happens. Too many disappointments.

He's going to get one big one soon.

Charlene   Why?

Deelie   You're going to find out sooner or later. His mam and dad might be getting a divorce.

Charlene   Why? What's 'appened?

Deelie   She seemed very clear about it all, really. We went and sat out in the quadrangle. They've got it nice. Bit of a shrubbery, and seats to sit down. Talked about things.

They've just . . . come to the end of it, I suppose.

Charlene   Another woman?

Deelie   Why do you say that?

Charlene   The way he is. Is it?

Deelie   You're a better judge than I thought.

Pause.

Charlene   Is that . . . why she tried to cut herself?

Deelie   You wouldn't believe the difference. Talking now as if a separation is the best thing for both of them. She even told me it was her idea to get the divorce. I've not seen her so positive for months.

Charlene   So what's going to happen to David?

Uncle Robert *comes in, paper in hand.* **Charlene** *goes into the kitchen. He reads:*

Robert   'And so our two idle apprentices move with the great tide on towards the race course.

'Lunatics, laughter, grand procession of the Grand Alliance Circus in all its splendour. Up the High Street, Bennetthorpe and out into the racecourse itself and the great sporting anniversary of the St Leger.'

Charlene *comes in with a cup of tea for* **Deelie.**

Charlene   All right?

Deelie (*to* **Charlene**)   Thank you.

Scene Ten

Waste land. **Charlene**, **Wink**, **Gobbo**, **David.**

Charlene *presents a play for* **David**. *She is with* **Wink**. **Gobbo** *stands some way off. He looks like he's spent months in the woods. His trouser legs are a concertina up to his knees with creases.*

Charlene   'What's gone on, Wilkie?'

Wink   'Nowt's gone on, Mrs Dickens.'

Charlene   'Something has. He's changed. He's so cold towards me. Ever since he came back to London.'

Wink   'Yeah, well, you know what a moody bugger 'e can be when 'e's on wi' a new book.'

Charlene   'He's having an affair, isn't he?'

Wink   'Give over. Course 'e int.'

Charlene   'Are you sure?'

Wink   'My dear Mrs Dickens, you 'ave my word.'

Charlene   As a gentleman.

Wink   'As an officer and a gentleman.'

Charlene (*to* **Gobbo**)   And now you come in.

Gobbo *moves over to them.*

Charlene   'You're seeing somebody, aren't you?'

Gobbo (*to* **Wink**)   'You cunt, you've gone and told 'er.'

Charlene 'You cad,' I said!

Gobbo 'You cad.'

Wink 'Yeah, well, you're wrong, then, 'cos I 'aven't. But she's guessed it.'

Charlene 'Who is she?'

Gobbo 'This girl what I picked up in Donny.'

Charlene 'I knew it. Oh, my heart is breaking with the pain of it.'

And you go, 'She's eighteen.'

Gobbo 'She's eighteen.'

Charlene 'You have a daughter older than that! You vile, wicked old letch. How could you? I that have bore you loads of kids and never a look at another man. Get out!'

Gobbo *makes to go.*

No. Not yet. You go, 'Can I have a divorce?'

Gobbo 'Can I have a divorce?'

Wink 'You cad, Dickens.'

Gobbo What *is* a cad, then?

Wink It's a posh cunt.

Gobbo Oh.

Wink And I smack you in the face with my glove and we 'ave a duel in the woods.

Charlene That's not in it.

Wink I know, be good, though. (*To* **Gobbo**.) 'Pistols at ten paces.'

Gobbo No.

Wink Yeah.

Gobbo What if I want a sword fight instead, then?

Charlene   Shut it. It's David's bit now. (*To* **Gobbo**.) You go out.

Wink   What do I do?

Charlene   You can go and get me a drink of water.

Wink   Right.

He moves off.

Gobbo   Can you get me one as well?

Charlene (*to* **Wink**)   Where you going?

Wink   Eh? Are you Charlene or Mrs Dickens?

Charlene   What?

Wink   Do you want a real drink?

Charlene   No.

Wink   I knew that. (*To* **Gobbo**.) You didn't, you plonk.

Gobbo   I did.

Charlene   Quiet backstage, please. (*To* **David**.) And . . . action. Come on.

Wink *and* **Gobbo** *look on, becoming enthralled.*

David   'Are you all right, Mum?'

Charlene   'Never better, son. Do not distress yourself. Your father has left us, but no matter, for even if he were to see the error of his ways, I would not have him back. We will survive without him, you and I. We will be strong and not let this be our ruin. I might yet meet someone else. A decent, honourable man. A kind man. Someone who will love me as I am and not want to make me into what he wants. And you, son, will one day meet someone nice.'

Pause.

Wink *prompts softly – a genuinely felt line:*

Wink   'I will never leave you, Mother.'

Gobbo *looks at him, impressed.*

David   'I will never leave you, Mother.'

Charlene   'You must, son. One day you will have to make your own way into the cruel world. But you will make it a kinder one, I know.'

She takes his hand in hers, kisses it. And now herself.

OK, Gobbo, thanks.

Gobbo (*to* **Wink**)   Can't I stay out a bit longer?

Wink   No.

Wink *comes forward with a blindfold, places it around* **Charlene***'s head.*

Charlene   I'm sick of doin' this every time you bring 'im out of 'is 'ole and put 'im back. When am I going to see where 'e lives?

Wink   I'm not showin' it you. All right? I'm not tellin' anybody. It's strictly club members only. You can saw my arm off with a frozen bread knife, if you like – and that bloody 'urts because I nearly done it as an accident on myself – I still wouldn't tell you. I'm trained to be tortured and not say owt.

Charlene   I'm supposed to be your friend, aren't I?

Wink   Sometimes.

Charlene   What do you mean, 'sometimes'? When 'ave I ever not been?

Wink   It's no use tryin' to confuse me. It won't work. It's a trade secret, innit? You might accidentally sprag.

Charlene   I won't.

Wink   Can you see?

Charlene   No.

He pretends to grope her breasts.

Charlene   Don't, Wink, I know what you're doin'.

Wink   You're a cheat, you're looking!

Charlene   I'm not.

Wink   Close your eyes, then.

(*To* **David**.) OK, take 'im back.

Gobbo   See you, Charlene.

Charlene   See you, Gobbo.

David *and* **Gobbo** *go off.*

Charlene   'Ave you told 'im about 'is Nanna?

Wink   What, getting' a brick through their window?

Charlene   Yeah.

Wink   No.

Charlene   Are you goin' to?

Wink   Yeah, but not now. After.

Charlene   After what?

Wink   After he's allowed 'ome.

Charlene   'Ave you seen 'er?

Wink   I told 'er we were campin' in our back yard.

Charlene   She thinks 'e's run away.

Wink   Everybody does.

Charlene   She's frightened for 'im, Wink.

Wink   Yeah. Me an' all.

I know who started it, you know.

Charlene   Started what?

Wink   Sayin' stuff. 'Im and the little girl.

Charlene   Who?

Wink   You know.

Charlene   No, I don't.

Wink   I don't care if 'e is your dad, e's a bastard twat and one day I'm goin' to creep up and commando 'im.

Charlene   Who says it's my dad?

Wink   I've got a spy in your 'ouse, aven't I?

Charlene   What's he said?

Wink   Enough.

Charlene   Don't do anything stupid, Wink.

Wink   As if.

David says 'e's off 'ome at the weekend. Is 'e?

Charlene   'E starts school next week.

Wink   'E wants to stay 'ere.

Charlene   Yeah, well, things are a bit . . . not good.

Wink   I'd love it, me. Posh 'ouse. Dead big garden, you could even 'ave your own fishin' pond.

Charlene   I mean between 'is mam and dad.

Wink   Why, what's up?

Charlene   I'm not saying.

Wink   Is 'e in love with another lady?

Charlene   Who told you?

Wink   You did. Your play, weren't it?

Charlene   Shut up, then.

Wink (*shouting, off*)   Halt! Who goes there, friend or foe?

David (*off*)   It's me.

Wink 'Ave you thought of a password yet?

David (*off*)   No.

David *appears.*

Wink   We ought to 'ave one.

He takes the blindfold off **Charlene**.

Charlene   You can't keep 'im there much longer, Wink. He stinks.

Wink   I'm a survival expert. 'E stays as long as I decide 'e needs to.

Charlene   What do I tell 'is nanna?

Wink   Tell 'er 'e's safe wi' me.

Charlene   What, 'Don't worry, Wink's put 'im in an 'ole in the ground somewhere'?

Wink   What's up wi' that?

You put me in a cupboard.

Charlene   When?

Wink   When I was Wilkie Collins.

Charlene   That was a play.

Wink   Yeah, but if we 'ad a real cupboard you would 've put me in it, wunt you?

Charlene   'E can't stay there!

Wink   'E stays till they find the girl and that man.

Charlene   What man?

Wink   The man what might've done it. 'E knows. (**David**.)

Charlene   What? What do you know?

Wink   The police've got all the information now, so they can do a computer check and then do a raid on 'is 'ouse wi' guns and CS gas.

Charlene (*to* **David**)   What's 'e on about?

But **David** *can't respond.*

Wink   We've told the police.

Charlene (*to* **David**)   You 'ave?

You saw a man with the girl?

David   No, not with the girl.

Wink   And they've put it on their computer. (*To* **David**.) 'Aven't they?

David   I suppose.

Wink   So when they get the girl back, Gobbo can come out and be normal.

Charlene (*to* **David**)   You've been to the police?

David *can't respond.*

Wink   What? What you done? Where's the log book? What you done with it?

Charlene   Log book?

Wink   Where is it?

David   I lost it.

Wink   Lost it?!

David   I was going to tell you.

Wink   What's 'appened?

David   I think it dropped out of my back pocket.

Wink   'Ow? Where?

David   I went back everywhere to look, but it wasn't there. Somebody must've picked it up.

Wink   You're lying.

David   I'm not.

Wink   Swear on Gobbo's life, then.

David   No.

Wink (*to* **Charlene**)   'E's lyin'. (*To* **David**.) All right, then, do a lie-detector test.

Charlene   Leave 'im, Wink.

Wink   What? A proper one, I mean. I've got one at 'ome.

Charlene   You 'aven't.

Wink   I 'ave, then! I got it last Christmas. It's like a red thing, and you put it on your 'and, an' you ask a question an' if you're lying it curls up.

Or do you want a red 'ot poker up your arse?

Charlene   You touch 'im if you dare!

Wink (*backing down*)   'E thinks I'm talking about real pokers. Yeah, well, I meant them what grow in gardens, din't I? Dint you know that?

David   Yes.

Wink   You're a liar. You tell me what 'appened to our log book, or else!

Charlene   Or else what?

Wink   Or I think of something, right?

(*To* **Charlene**.) I tell 'im what you told me.

David   What about?

Charlene   Wink. Stop it.

Wink (*to* **David**)   Ask 'er why we did that play.

Charlene   Shut it.

Wink (*to* **David**)   Go on, ask 'er.

Charlene   I mean it. Don't you dare.

David   What's he talking about?

Charlene   Nothin'.

Wink   You know Mrs Dickens?

David   What about her?

Charlene (*to* **Wink**)   I'll kill you. I won't talk to you ever.

Wink   It's your mum.

David   What's he talking about?

Charlene   Just tell 'im!

David   My Aunt Deelie's got it only she won't give it back.

Charlene   Green exercise book?

David   Yes.

Wink   You got it?

Charlene   No.

(*To* **David**.) My dad found 'er with it last night. 'E took it off 'er.

Wink   Bastard! The fucker!

David (*to* **Charlene**)   What does he mean about my mum?

Wink   That's it, then. Gobbo's last chance gone. What do we do now?

David   Charlene? What does he mean?

Scene Eleven

Aunt Deelie'*s house.*

David *is with* **Charlene**, *who is stuffing his pockets with cheese triangles, bread, biscuits she has just taken from the kitchen.* **Deelie** *comes in from the hall, hands* **David** *a five pound note.*

Deelie   Get something for him in the shop with this.

David   Thank you.

Deelie   Something substantial. Not snacks.

David   OK.

Deelie   He wants a hot meal inside him. Get him a meat pie.

(*To* **Charlene**.) When your dad's out the way you can warm it through. I'll do him a bit of veg.

David   He had some chips last night.

Deelie   Good. I don't want him going hungry.

Charlene   'E's not likely to do that now you're sendin' 'im food parcels.

Deelie   Well, what am I supposed to do? You tell me he's hiding away somewhere, I'd visions of him in some derelict house eating nothing but Mars Bars and crisps.

Uncle Robert *approaches, singing. He comes in with* **David**'s *book.*

Robert   Well, I 'ave to say, it's very thorough. 'Daily Observations of a Man in the Park.' Eh? Very well presented.

You must've spent 'ours up there, eh? The private investigator and his assistants Lone Ranger and Tonto.

And you thought you'd pass it on to your Auntie Deelie. What for?

(*To* **Aunt Deelie**.) For you to pass on to the police?

Deelie   Don't be ridiculous.

Robert   Don't say that to me, say it to 'im. (*To* **David**.) Ridiculous, she says. No intention of givin' it to the police. (*To* **Aunt Deelie**.) Or 'ad you?

David   Please can I have it back?

Robert   Top secret. Best keep it somewhere safe. Can't leave such a vital document lying about, when it's been compiled by 'onest, reliable witnesses, can we?

I mean, if we wanted a straightforward, honest statement from a member of the public, where could we do better than to go to one of your friends, eh?

Deelie   All right, you've made your point. Don't make him feel –

Robert   They'll be very keen to act on it, I'm sure. They'll probably want you to go down and answer a few questions about it. That'll make you feel important, won't it, Master Davy?

Deelie   Why do you do it? Why do you always have to make people feel foolish?

Robert   You do that without my 'elp.

Deelie   Is it necessary? Is it?

Robert   Would you've taken it?

Aunt Deelie *can't answer.*

No, because you know what a bloody fool you'd look if you did.

Deelie   He's just a boy.

Robert   And 'e trusted you to take it.

And now 'e knows you can't be trusted.

He goes off to his shed with the book.

Deelie   I'm sorry, David.

David   They wanted me to help them and I said I would because they're my friends, and now I've let them down.

Deelie   They'll find her soon.

Pause.

Deelie   They didn't want him. Palmed him on to his grandmother at six. She loved him to bits.

She once said to me, 'If I had a pound for every time he's come crying to me and broke my heart with what's been said and done to him, I'd be rich enough to buy us a house a million miles away from this place.'

I said, 'Would you move from round here?'

'Just give me chance,' she said.

Charlene (*to* **David**)   'E used to spit on woodlice. The kids in the street got 'im for it one day, 'eld 'im down while they phlegmed on 'is face. 'E went 'ome all green slime.

Robert (*off*)   Bastard!

Deelie (*to* **Charlene**)   Now what?

Robert *bursts in.*

Robert   Oh, the dirty bastard! The filthy little rag-arsed gippo! Eeagh! The stink! Bloody everywhere!

Deelie (*getting up*)   What?

Robert   Shit! Some dirty little sod gone and broke in and shit all over my shed! It looks like it's been saved up for a week! Everywhere! Wipin' is arse on all my papers, all my work. Months! There's a bloody turd as long as my arm sittin' on my typewriter!

Deelie   Well, at least he didn't steal it.

Robert   Oh well, that's all right, then, innit? 'Ow the bloody 'ell can I use it! 'E might as well 've nicked it for all the bloody use it is now. Or do you want I should pick it off wi' a pair of fireside tongs!

Deelie   I'm just saying.

Robert   Well, don't bother, less you can say summat useful. What the 'ell 'am I gunna do about my papers? Shit and piss, it's ruined! All that bloody work! My magnum opus.

Deelie   You've a copy, haven't you?

Robert   No.

Deelie   I thought you sent one off?

Robert   I've revised it since then, 'aven't I? Refined it. Fine-tuned it.

Deelie   Can't you remember it?

Robert   Don't talk stupid!

Deelie   Well, can't you get them to give you back what you've done and work from that?

Robert   In two days?

Deelie   It's better than nothing, isn't it?

Robert   Just . . . just let me think, will you? You've got no idea, 'ave you? It's the defilin', innit? I'm defiled, 'ere!

Deelie   What?

Robert   Never mind. No use talkin' to you about it, what would you know?

Deelie   So has anything been taken?

Robert   I don't bloody know, do I? I were gaggin' soon as I stepped in.

Deelie *goes out.*

Robert (*to* **Charlene**)   This is your bloody gippos for you.

Charlene   Yeah, I suppose.

Robert   Why do that, though? What 'ave I done? Eh?

Charlene   I don't know.

Robert   Nothin'. I've said nowt to none of 'em. Live and let live, that's me. I mean, it's a bloody right tip down where they are, but 'ave I complained like some folk?

Just 'appened to be my shed. Nowt in it of any consequence – not to them, anyroad. Nothin' to flog, see. Probably narked because they'd broke in and found nowt worth stealin'.

Charlene   Probably.

Robert   Wiped 'is arse on my Dickens. Some greasy little sneak-thief peasant without a clue. No notion of its literary worth; it's value as to the unique contribution it was about to make; it's explosive contents.

Charlene   You're not goin' to get your copy back, then?

Robert   Will I get it to the piece of art it was, though, in time?

Charlene   Course you will.

Uncle Robert *sits down.*

Charlene   You leavin' my mam to clean it up?

Robert   No.

Charlene   What you doin', then?

Robert   I'm stocktakin'. (*He taps his head.*) In 'ere. Assessin' the damage.

I'm puttin' down your push-bike for a start.

Charlene   I got rid of that ages ago.

Robert   They don't know that, do they?

Charlene   You can't do that.

Robert   Course I can. I won't get no compensation for the mental disturbance, for the intellectual property, will I? For the labour of love?

Lawnmower.

Charlene   We 'aven't a lawn.

Robert   I'll 'ave to inform the police.

(*To* **David**.) We can give 'em your book when they come round.

Charlene   Dad. Stop teasin' im. You're not goin' to do anythin' with it. He knows that.

Robert Why not?

Charlene You know why not.

Robert A tale told by an idiot, you mean?

Diary of a goon that likes little girls? Gone on the run?

Charlene It's not like that.

Robert Well, what is it like, then?

'Ad you fooled.

Charlene Don't. Please, Dad.

Robert 'I'll show you mine if you show me yours.'

Charlene We were kids!

Robert 'E was fourteen!

Charlene Yeah, fourteen goin' on four.

Robert The dirty little bugger.

Charlene 'Ow do you know it wasn't my idea?

Robert Eh? You can leave that alone. Right now.

Charlene It might've been. I can't remember.

Robert Don't talk stupid. You were six year old! 'E's a wrong un. 'E was then, 'e is now.

'E knows I bloody know it, an all.

'You nasty man.'

In fact . . .

Charlene He's got nothing to do with the girl.

Robert Never mind bloody gippos. Some little shitty-arsed perv in my shed. Eh? The little bastard.

(*To* **David**.) You know owt about it?

David No.

Robert (*to* **Charlene**)   You?

David   It weren't 'im. It weren't 'im!

Scene Twelve

Waste land. **Aunt Deelie** *arrives, in her Spar shop uniform. She carries a food parcel. She begins to talk to the unseen* **Gobbo**.

Deelie   They found the girl and her dad in a caravan in Skegness.

I think they're organising a street party tonight.

I popped in to see your nan this morning, see if she needed anything.

Only for you to come home.

A twig snaps.

Wink (*off, softly*)   Bollocks.

Deelie   You can come out now. It's safe.

Nobody's going to get you. I'll walk home with you, if you want me to.

She sits down.

Not done this in a long time. Daisy chains after dinner on the school field. That's a long time ago, isn't it?

I'm still here. If you need me.

I haven't forgotten my boyfriend.

I still have a picture someone drew for me. A trip to the zoo. There's me and you and an elephant. With love. I keep it inside a cookery book.

Last night of the fair tomorrow. I know you like fairs. Toffee apples.

I'm worried about you.

Out here all night. The shed's cleaned out. I suppose David told you he thinks it's you. I've told him, if he ever touches you . . . He knows what I'll do if he does.

I might anyway. One of these days.

'His papers.' 'His talk.' 'All the extra work.'

He doesn't know I found a letter they sent him. Thank you very much but no thanks. He daren't tell me. What would that do to his pride?

David *arrives, with* **Charlene**.

Charlene   You told him about the girl?

Deelie   If he was listening.

Wink *suddenly appears from the undergrowth, makes for* **David**.

Wink (*to* **David**)   You spragger. You bloody spragger, you went and told it was us in 'is shed!

Charlene   He's not said anything!

Wink   Your dad come down 'ere gunna kill Gobbo. 'E couldn't find 'im, though, could 'e? 'E was shoutin' 'e was goin' to get us both done!

Charlene   They've found the girl.

Wink   Too late! It's too late for that.

Wink *looks at the food parcel.*

Wink   Waste of time. 'E's gone.

Charlene   Where?

Wink   Yeah, sure. As if. I'm sayin' nothin'. Not wi' this bloody grasser to 'ear.

David   I never told him anything.

Wink   If you'd done what we said and gone to the police –

Deelie   It wouldn't have made things happen any quicker.

Wink   It would. How do you know? You never give it 'em, did you?

Deelie   Look, it's done. Where −?

Wink   You never did nowt about it, did you? Dint you believe us?

Deelie   It's not about not believing you. Where is he?

Wink   You was a nice lady. You was the one in everybody we could trust and you went and never believed us, 'cause your 'usband told you not to.

Deelie   No, that's not −

Wink   You're one of them lot. We thought you was one of us but you're just a spy, aren't you?

Deelie   No.

Wink   Yeah. I'm tellin' you nothin', so you can go back and tell 'im Wink says to go and fuck 'imself.

Charlene   Wink −

Deelie   You don't use words like that to me. You know better than that.

Wink   Who do you think you are, eh?

Charlene   Wink, stop it now.

Wink   I'll say what I want. I'm not at school any more. Go on, fuck off.

Aunt Deelie *looks at him a moment, crushed, turns and walks off.*

Charlene   Mum . . .

She steps across to **Wink***, smacks him in the face.* **Wink** *takes it, as ever, and then starts to cry.*

Wink   He was my best friend. And 'e thinks 'e's dead.

(*To* **David**.) We was all right till you come.

Why don't you go back 'ome?

David   I am this weekend.

Wink   Your mum comin' ome?

David   It's very likely.

Wink   She's not a loony any more, then?

David   She's not loony.

Wink   She's a Gong Donkey.

Charlene   Wink. Stop it.

And I know why.

David   No, you don't.

Wink   I do, then.

Charlene   Shurrup, Wink. I mean it. You say anythin', an I won't ever be mates again.

Wink   I won't be 'ere to be mates. I'm off after Gobbo.

Charlene   Where?

Wink (*to* **David**)   You made 'er loony.

David   My mother's not a loony.

Charlene   Wink, what d'you mean, 'You're after Gobbo'?

Wink (*to* **David**)   You and your dad sent 'er bonkers makin' up stories, tellin' lies all the time.

David   I don't make up stories. What, like about your dad in the SAS?

Wink   That's true!

David   He was on the dole and he took one look at you and left!

Wink   You're stupid.

Charlene (*to* **David**)   Who told you that? My dad?

Wink   He was an SAS 'ero.

Charlene   Take no notice. It's somethin' my dad's told 'im.

David   He walked out because you're a Gong Donkey and your mum went on the bottle.

Wink   You're not to say that. I've got 'is book.

David   Anybody could've written that.

Charlene   Shut up, will you? Just shut up!

Wink   It's got 'is name writ on it.

David   You put it on.

Wink   I never!

Charlene   Wink, listen. That's all my dad telling him stuff. It's my dad. He's all mouth. You don't 'ave to go anywhere.

Wink (*to* **David**)   She's leavin' you.

David   What?

Charlene   Wink, please don't. Where you goin'?

David   What do you mean?

Wink (*to* **Charlene**)   I told you, I'm off wi' Gobbo.

Charlene   Where?

Wink *gets his bearings, points.*

Wink   West north west. I think 'e's gone up river to a cave we found once, only I'm not tellin' where. I'm not tellin' any of you. I've got to find 'im because I've got us both jobs, see. I've seen a man this mornin'. Said we can start tonight. Proper jobs. As long as we want, 'cause we're off to convoy next week. It's another place miles away. Earning loads of money, see. So we won't be 'ere to be beaten up no more. I'm gonna smoke my pipe whenever I want and I'm 'avin a tiger tattooed on my arm. You get to whirligig the lasses if you want, an' all.

Charlene   What?

Wink   Stuff all this.

Charlene   Wink, you can't just go. I mean your mam and that. You can't leave 'er.

Wink   She dunt even know I'm 'ere.

Charlene   Who's goin' to look after 'er?

Wink   I don't 'ave to dress 'er an' undress 'er any more and put 'er to bed. She lives on the sofa.

Charlene   You love 'er, Wink.

Wink   Yeah? So? I'll send 'er some wages.

Charlene   What about Gobbo's grandma? And your paper round ?

Wink   You tell 'em. (*To* **David**.) And no followin', you.

He picks up the food parcel.

Charlene   Don't go like this.

David (*fighting back tears*)   My mother is not a loony and she's not leaving us.

Charlene   Wink. Please. Not like this.

Wink   Tell 'im to stop making faces, then. It makes me feel funny. (*To* **David**.) I go like Incredible 'Ulk sometimes. (*To* **Charlene**.) Don't I?

(*Shouting off, to* **Aunt Deelie**.) I'm sorry, Mrs Alverley! I'm sorry for that word!

(*To* **Charlene**.) Will you tell 'er?

Charlene   Yes.

Wink (*to* **David**)   My mam *is* a drunk. I let 'er 'it me, but it just makes 'er 'ate me for not 'ittin' 'er back, like my dad did. I'm not a man like 'e was, I'm a waste of space. She keeps sayin' for me to go and good riddance, so I might as well.

Charlene   What about me? What about us, and that?

Wink   You only want me for acting in your plays.

Charlene   I don't.

Wink   Nobody else would do it, only me and Gobbo, and you only got 'im because 'e can do the 'andsome prince.

Charlene   What? It's just a game. We don't –

Wink   I know I'm thick, but I'm not that thick. I know you do it with us to practise on when you get a proper boyfriend. I know that much.

He realises he's hurt her, backtracks.

Why don't you go on the chat room? (*To* **David**.) 'E says they've got computers in the library. (*To* **Charlene**.) Get one that way.

Charlene   Yeah.

Wink   See you, Charlene.

Charlene   See you, Wink. Tell Gobbo . . .

Wink   What?

Charlene   Just tell 'im I won't ever forget 'im.

Wink   I won't.

I will, I mean.

What did you say, again?

Charlene   See you, Wink.

Wink   Yeah. See you.

Wink *goes off. They watch him.* **Charlene** *is tearful.*

David   I want to go home.

Charlene   You will be. Tomorrow.

And if you're not, you can come to the fair with us.

Pause.

David   There isn't a cave. He only said it because I told him about one in a book.

Scene Thirteen

Aunt Deelie's *house. Saturday night.*

David *sits reading.* **Aunt Deelie** *with him, anxious.*

Deelie   He might have had to go out on an emergency call.

It'll be murder in town.

You could've gone to the fair tonight after all. I said you would have plenty of time.

David   Sometime after eight, he said.

Deelie   Maybe he wanted to stay with your mum a bit, settle her down. All that anticipating and then to tell her she's not well enough. They should never have told her beforehand she might be coming out.

David   I'll see her tomorrow at the hospital, before I catch the train back to school.

Deelie   Yes. Whatever happens . . . She loves you. You know that, don't you?

David   Yes.

Deelie   More than you will ever know.

David   I know.

Deelie   It's been lovely having you here. Could've been better for you, I know. One thing and another. I've got used to it, I suppose. You live with them, but you don't see just how . . . the way things really are, until you've got company.

I'll miss your company.

He smiles at her.

I will. It won't be the same.

It's good that we can talk about things.

He goes back to his book.

Deelie   Is it a good book?

David   Quite good.

Deelie   Adventure story?

David   Yes.

Are there any caves round here?

Deelie   I don't know.

David   I might walk up the river one day.

Deelie   You can come back whenever you like.

David   Somebody said there might be caves up there.

Deelie   An expedition.

David   Yes.

Deelie   Adventure.

I wish you many of them, David.

David   Thank you.

Charlene *arrives. She carries a cuddly elephant.*

Charlene (*to* **David**)   You should've come.

Deelie   Good time?

Charlene   Brilliant. Some awesome rides. 'Onest. Dead scary, some of 'em. Loads throwin' up. I nearly did.

David   What did you go on?

Charlene   Only one I didn't were 'cause they were queuein' for miles.

Deelie   I don't know how you dare.

Charlene   I daren't. You 'ave to, though, it's great.

Deelie   What did you win this on?

Charlene   I was given it.

Deelie   Oh? That's nice.

Charlene   He gave it me to give to you.

She hands it to **Aunt Deelie**.

He said to tell you, thank you for bein' a nice lady.

David   Gobbo?

Deelie   He was there?

Charlene   They both were. Wink on the 'uck a duck, Gobbo at the bouncy castle with all the little kids.

Deelie   Really? They're all right?

Charlene   They're loving it.

David   They work there?

Charlene   They're goin' on wherever with them tomorrow.

Deelie   Were they surprised to see you?

Charlene   You should've seen 'em. They're dead 'appy, both of 'em. I'm dead pleased for 'em.

Deelie   Does anyone know where they are?

Charlene   They're safe. I've to give his grandma some money. Wink's mum too.

David   They get paid?

Charlene   They got four pounds fifty between them yesterday morning just looking in the grass.

Deelie   The bouncy castle?

Charlene   Yes. He said to tell you he's a Catcher in the Rye now.

Deelie   A story I once told him.

David   That's all he ever wanted to be.

Uncle Robert *comes in. He's been drinking.*

Robert   Good evening, all. How sweet the homecoming welcome. And how did it go, dear father?

Recent, shall we say, 'difficulties' regarding soiled paper having been overcome, we gave a good account of ourselves. In short, Master Davy, a triumph.

And your visit to the St Leger Fair a night of wonder and amazement?

Charlene   What?

Robert   Spent up?

Charlene   Might 'ave.

Robert   What's Gypsy Rose got to tell you this time?

Was she there?

Did you ask for your money back?

What did she say, then, the man of your dreams got a bit delayed?

Charlene   She said I'm goin' to travel, if you must know.

Robert   Where to?

Charlene   As far away as I can get.

Robert (*to* **David**)   We've still got the pleasure of, then.

Must be on a home visit, eh? Sat by the bed. Or in it.

Deelie   Robert.

Robert   Can't even pick the lad up.

David   He'll be here in a minute. I'll bring my things down.

He gets up, goes off to the stairs. **Aunt Deelie** *watches him, concerned.*

Robert 'And how was your evening, dearest?' Delightful, my dove. The air electric with suspense as I wove my tale of intrigue.

Charlene (*to* **Aunt Deelie**)   Mum? Is everything all right?

Robert A little bladder relief.

He moves off.

Consequent to a certain imbibing in celebration of success, my dove. At which it was proposed a rendezvous in the stock room of a certain wallpaper warehouse.

He stops at the door, turns to them.

Otherwise known as the ghost room in 'The Two Robins'. Might even stay the night. It's on next month's agenda.

He goes off.

Charlene Mum?

Deelie Your Auntie Audrey went missing this afternoon.

Charlene Missing?

Deelie They found her. She's going to be all right.

They found her in a toilet in town working her way through a bottle of paracetamols.

I rang on the off-chance at tea time when they told me.

Charlene And she's all right?

Deelie 'They got her settled,' he said. I want to be there, not here, but what do I say to David?

Charlene Just say they want you at the shop.

Deelie What about where his dad is? Shall we just say it's some emergency?

Charlene I'll say it. You go.

David *comes through with his suitcase, backpack, a present.*

David (*to* **Aunt Deelie**)   Thank you for looking after me.

He hands her the present.

Deelie   You shouldn't have.

She opens the gift. It's perfume.

David   Charlene said you like the smell.

Deelie   Thank you. It's lovely.

Robert *comes in. He looks at the elephant.*

Robert (*to* **Charlene**)   So where's Dumbo goin', then? Wi' rest of your menagerie?

Charlene   It's not mine.

Robert (*to* **Aunt Deelie**)   What do you want summat like that for?

Charlene   It's a present.

Robert   It's a pink elephant. It's for a little girl, isn't it? (*To* **Aunt Deelie**.) What do you want with it?

Charlene   It's from an old boyfriend.

Deelie   Charlene . . .

Robert   What? 'Er?

Charlene   In memory of a kindness.

Robert (*to* **Aunt Deelie**)   First and last, weren't I, dearest? Eh? The one and only.

(*Leering over her in drunken affection.*) And likewise. Eyes for none but thee, my dove.

Deelie   Stop it.

Robert   Unlike Mr Dickens.

You could've 'eard a pin drop.

Deelie   Stop it!

Robert   Gasps of astonishment. 'Eighteen?!'

Deelie   For God's sake! Don't talk to me. Don't talk to me. Nobody cares!

Robert   What's she on about? What's up with you?

Deelie   Nobody is interested, not now, not ever. You never did it, Robert. You never went. They didn't want you. Nobody does. Go away. Just go away!

Robert   What's she on about?

Deelie   Go to bed.

Robert   Can't. Adrenalin still coursin' through.

Deelie   Your life is nothing but a made-up story!

Pause.

Robert   And when I look at what I've got to live with, I wonder why?

I'll make my own supper, then.

He goes into the kitchen.

Deelie   I think what I'll do . . .

David, I've got to go out. I'm covering. Somebody poorly.

I don't know what time your dad'll be here. You might be staying the night, eh?

Anyway. Bye, love.

Aunt Deelie *gets hold of* **David**, *gives him a hug.*

She goes out.

David   So will they be helping the men take down all the machines tonight?

Charlene   I expect so.

David   They won't have time to look in the grass for money, will they?

Charlene No.

David Anyway, they haven't got a torch.

Uncle Robert *comes through, eating a piece of bread, some cheese.*

Robert Where's your mother?

Charlene She's run away with the gypsies.

Robert Got the monk on, 'as she?

(*To* **David**, *by way of explanation.*) Stands at the gate, watchin' stars.

Or 'as she gone to bed?

Pickled onion.

He goes back through into the kitchen, humming a song to himself.
It might be 'Food Glorious Food'.

Charlene Wink says sorry.

David What for?

Charlene For what he said. He said to tell you he thought you were all right.

David Did he?

Charlene And next year's St Leger Fair, he's off to let you 'ave a free go on the 'uck a duck.

You'll be all right.

Your dad's probably out on some emergency, eh?

I'll just take these up. Out of his way.

She picks up the elephant, perfume, goes off.

David *puts down his suitcase, backpack, takes up his book and reads.*

The End.

Printed in the USA
CPSIA information can be obtained
at www.ICGtesting.com
LVHW020853171024
794056LV00002B/511